ON IDEAS

# ON IDEAS

## A PHILOSOPHICAL DIALOGUE

Nicholas J. Pappas

Algora Publishing
New York

Library of Congress Cataloging-in-Publication Data —

Names: Pappas, Nicholas J., author.
Title: On ideas : a philosophical dialogue / Nicholas J. Pappas.
Description: New York : Algora Publishing, 2020. | Summary: "A
   philosophical treatment of ideas, the book presents a dialogue
   much in the spirit of classical philosophical dialogues,
   notably those of Plato and Xenophon. As those authors do in a number of
   their works, Nick Pappas adopts a light and playful tone to treat a
   serious topic. This contrast helps bring out the truth, in an
   approachable style that requires no prior exposure to philosophy and
   heavy intellectual work"— Provided by publisher.
Identifiers: LCCN 2020002531 (print) | LCCN 2020002532 (ebook) | ISBN
   9781628944136 (trade paperback) | ISBN 9781628944143 (hardcover) | ISBN
   9781628944150 (pdf)
Subjects: LCSH: Idea (Philosophy) | Plato. | Xenophon.
Classification: LCC B105.I28 P37 2020 (print) | LCC B105.I28 (ebook) |
   DDC 121/.4—dc23
LC record available at https://lccn.loc.gov/2020002531
LC ebook record available at https://lccn.loc.gov/2020002532

## More Books by Nick Pappas
## from Algora Publishing

Controvert, or On the Lie and Other Philosophical Dialogues, 2008

Aristocrat, and The Community: Two Philosophical Dialogues, 2010

On Awareness: A Collection of Philosophical Dialogues, 2011

Belief and Integrity: Philosophical Dialogues, 2011

On Strength, 2012

On Freedom: A Philosophical Dialogue, 2014

On Life: Philosophical Dialogues, 2015

On Love: A Philosophical Dialogue, 2016

On Destiny: A Philosophical Dialogue, 2016

On Wisdom: A Philosophical Dialogue, 2017

All of Health: A Philosophical Dialogue, 2018

On Education: A Philosophical Dialogue, 2018

On Power: A Philosophical Dialogue, 2019

# INTRODUCTION

This book is a play about ideas. Professor states early on that "Every person on Earth is, in one way or another, an idea." This suggestion remains in the background throughout the conversation that follows. What does it mean to be an idea? We can be dominated, captured, by an idea. An idea can, on the other hand, animate us. What makes for the difference? Director, a philosopher, admits to a fear of being overwhelmed by ideas. Actor shows so much enthusiasm for ideas that he wants to continue the extensive conversation reported here over another meal later that same day.

We live in a nation of ideas, one founded on ideas. We value the free exchange of ideas. We even speak of a marketplace of ideas. If ideas weren't valuable to us, no such market could exist. But few of us question what an idea is. In some important ways, it seems self-evident. But try to give a satisfying answer to the question, "What is an idea?" I don't find it easy. That lack of ease prompted me to write this book.

The action is the characters' thought as represented in what they say. Their spoken words differ from the thoughts in their heart of hearts, though we can guess at what those thoughts might be from what they say. But this is not to criticize them. It means they're like us.

Ideas are related to thought. Director says: "Some people experience pain from thinking; and some people experience pleasure in thought." Perhaps it is more accurate to say all of us experience one or the other from time to time. But do we cherish ideas that bring us pleasure, and reject ideas that make us work? Then again, why assume that work here is unpleasant? Maybe we do so because pleasure in thinking is an acquired taste, born of wrestling with difficult ideas.

There is no necessary contradiction in taking pleasure in serious things. Serious effort can even be fun. In a way, this is why I wrote this book with

1

a light and comic tone. That doesn't change the fact that I gave as much serious thought to the ideas presented here as I have it in me to give. Contrast helps bring out the truth.

In closing, I will confess to a desire I have. I wish that someone who reads and profits from this book might one day write the sequel, the dinner conversation the characters promise at the end. I would very much like this because I feel there's more to be said about ideas. I do not claim to have treated the topic exhaustively. In fact, it's hard to see how anyone can treat the topic exhaustively. After all, if Professor is right and we're all ideas, what would we have to say about ourselves in such a treatment?

Still, I'd like someone to go further than I have here. And that would certainly make me think.

I hope you enjoy the book.

Nick Pappas

Scene

*Wednesday morning, over breakfast at an off-campus restaurant*

1

*Actor:* There are only two types of ideas—good and bad.

*Director:* What's a bad idea?

*Actor:* You'll know by the results.

*Director:* I suppose that's how you'll know the good ones, too.

*Actor:* Yes.

*Professor:* So if you take a job on a film, and you have a wonderful time making it, and you develop friendships that will last a lifetime, but the movie doesn't bring in much money—was it a bad idea to have taken the job?

*Actor:* An idea can be good for some things but bad for others.

*Director:* So you have to rank the importance of the various things and decide whether the idea is more good than bad?

*Actor:* Exactly. And in Professor's example there was more good than bad.

*Professor:* But then there are more than two types of ideas.

*Actor:* How so?

*Professor:* There are ideas that are one hundred percent good; there are ideas that are, let's say, eighty percent good. There are ideas that are one hundred percent bad; there are ideas that are fifty percent bad. And so on.

*Director:* Yes, but how do we know?

*Actor:* Know what?

*Director:* If you decide an idea is mostly bad and don't act on it, you'll know it was bad... how?

*Actor:* You know when you see someone else who acts on it coming to harm.

*Director:* I see. Ideas are bad because they bring someone, anyone, harm.

*Actor:* Right.

*Director:* But what about things that bring harm to others but benefit to you?

*Actor:* Well, it's bad to harm others.

*Director:* Even if we're at war? Don't you want to benefit yourself and your friends and harm the enemy? Aren't wars filled with good ideas like this?

*Actor:* Yes, wars are filled with ideas like that.

*Director:* So an idea isn't bad just because it brings harm.

*Actor:* Apparently not. But we know it's bad if it brings no good.

### 2

*Professor:* Good ideas do more good than harm to everyone involved.

*Director:* Yes, that sounds good. But, again, what about in war? What if we, for example, who are small in number, have an idea that will work harm on a much greater number, our enemies? Is it a good idea?

*Professor:* If our cause is just, numbers don't matter.

*Director:* Ah. So the goodness of ideas depends on justice? Just ideas are good; unjust ideas are bad?

*Actor:* Maybe in war. But there are so many everyday ideas. They don't depend on justice.

*Director:* Give us an example of an everyday idea.

*Actor:* You have to decide if it's a good idea to skip work to spend time with an old friend who's only in town for a day.

*Professor:* I take it you'll be missing something important at work?

*Actor:* Yes.

*Professor:* Well, it depends what you want.

*Director:* Ideas are good when they give us what we want?

*Professor:* Do you think they're good when they don't?

*Actor:* We want to see our friend but don't want trouble at work.

*Director:* We want it both ways.

*Actor:* We almost always do.

*Professor:* Speak for yourself.

*Director:* Hmm. I think there's another idea in play that we should examine.

*Actor:* What idea?

*Director:* That the things we want are mutually exclusive. They might not be. There might a third way here.

*Actor:* Exactly! And I think it's fair to say that mutual exclusion is almost always a bad idea.

*Director:* Because anything is possible?

*Actor:* Yes.

*Director:* Good things are possible; bad things are possible.

*Actor:* This idea focuses on the good.

*Director:* So is the idea more properly put as 'everything good is possible'?

*Actor:* Why not?

*Director:* And then everything bad is impossible?

*Actor:* Now you're being ridiculous.

*Director:* The bad is possible?

*Actor:* Of course.

*Director:* But the good is possible.

*Actor:* You know it is.

*Director:* Is there anything we're leaving out of the possible?

*Professor:* The neither good nor bad.

*Director:* The neutral?

*Professor:* Yes, so many neutral things are possible.

*Director:* Good things are possible. Bad things are possible. Neutral things are possible. Anything is possible.

*Professor:* Right. But the interesting question is—how do these things rank?

*Actor:* I say it's good, neutral, anything, bad.

*Director:* Professor?

*Professor:* Neutral, anything, good, bad.

*Actor:* How can you rank neutral and anything above good?

*Professor:* Good always brings its proper bad.

*Actor:* You believe in a zero sum world? Good for me is bad for you?

*Professor:* Maybe not for me, no. But for someone.

*Actor:* Director, do you believe that?

*Director:* No. But I'd like to hear Professor explain.

### 3

*Professor:* Consider this. Suppose I'm handsome.

*Director:* Please don't tax our imaginations so early in the morning.

*Professor:* Is it good to be handsome?

*Actor:* It is.

*Professor:* Then consider further. I'm handsome—until you come along, you who are more handsome than I.

*Actor:* But you'd still be handsome.

*Professor:* But what if I'm the most handsome in my set, until you come along? Do you agree it's good to be the most handsome?

*Actor:* Well....

*Professor:* Oh, that's alright. You don't have to agree to get the point.

*Actor:* Let's say I agree.

*Professor:* Good. Now, the good for you—being most handsome—is bad for me, because I'm no longer most handsome. That's easily understood, isn't it?

*Actor:* It is. But you think all good is like this?

*Professor:* In one way or another? Yes.

*Actor:* I really don't agree.

*Director:* Professor, I'm having trouble understanding.

*Professor:* What's the trouble?

*Director:* What's the good of being handsome?

*Professor:* We should let Actor answer.

*Actor:* People are attracted to you.

*Director:* That's it? That's what's good about being handsome?

*Actor:* I know what you mean. What counts is what you do with the attractions.

*Director:* What can be done?

*Actor:* Anything.

*Director:* I don't believe it.

*Actor:* Why not?

*Director:* Because certain things of 'anything' will render you ugly.

*Actor:* To some.

*Director:* There are those who will overlook ugliness because of... looks?

*Actor:* Of course.

*Director:* Professor, would you?

*Professor:* I wouldn't.

*Director:* What does it mean when one person looks at another and says 'beautiful' and someone else looks and says 'ugly'?

*Actor:* It means opinions vary.

*Director:* What about the ideas of ugly and beautiful? Do they vary?

*Actor:* No, they don't. They always mean what they mean.

*Director:* Do all ideas always mean what they mean?

*Actor:* I think they do.

*Director:* But we don't all agree on where they apply.

*Actor:* No, we don't.

*Director:* 'Handsome' is an idea.

*Professor:* Of course handsome is an idea. All adjectives are ideas—all nouns, too.

*Actor:* What about pronouns?

*Professor:* Ideas one and all.

*Actor:* So 'I', 'you', 'he', 'she', 'we', 'they'—all ideas?

*Professor:* All ideas.

*Director:* What about the people they represent? Ideas?

*Professor:* Every person on Earth is, in one way or another, an idea.

*Actor:* And some are more interesting than others.

*Director:* Why wouldn't everyone select a more interesting idea?

*Actor:* Not all of us have the choice.

*Director:* Why not?

*Actor:* Because we're given our ideas by others.

*Director:* What would it take to break from them?

*Actor:* A terrible struggle.

*Director:* How do we succeed?

*Actor:* By being true to an idea of our choosing.

*Director:* How do we know we're true?

*Actor:* We live without contradiction.

*Professor:* And if others see contradiction?

*Actor:* We can't let that derail us.

*Professor:* We're a train traveling down tracks we ourselves lay.

*Actor:* Yes, exactly.

*Director:* Who clears the land for the tracks?

*Actor:* Ideally? We do.

*Director:* And less than ideally?

*Actor:* We lay our tracks where others have cleared the way.

*Director:* And if we all clear our own way and travel that way?

*Actor:* Then good for you in no way means bad for me.

### 4

*Professor:* I'm not sure that follows.

*Director:* Maybe it doesn't. But why is the ideal for us to do the clearing ourselves?

*Actor:* Because if you clear your own way, you're more original.

*Professor:* Ah, originality. What a wonderful idea.

*Actor:* It's not an idea—it's a fact.

*Professor:* Facts aren't ideas?

*Actor:* How could they be?

*Professor:* It was a fact that the Earth was flat. That was the idea.

*Actor:* And you'd say it's only an idea that the Earth is round?

*Professor:* 'Only' an idea? I think you underestimate the power of ideas.

*Actor:* You underestimate the power of facts.

*Professor:* Like the power of the fact that you're the most handsome one here? Or is that an opinion?

*Actor:* It's an opinion.

*Professor:* You say that out of modesty.

*Director:* What does it matter why he said it? The fact is, he said it. It's his opinion. And opinions are facts.

*Actor:* Let me guess. It's a fact that in your opinion I'm handsome.

*Director:* Yes, but you'll want to know what my idea of handsome is.

*Actor:* What is it?

*Director:* I think I'll hold that over you.

*Actor:* Keep me wondering?

*Director:* Yes, and the more you wonder the more handsome I think you'll be.

*Professor:* Why?

*Director:* Because philosophy is born of wonder.

*Actor:* So a philosopher, any philosopher, is more handsome to you than me?

*Director:* More beautiful, yes.

*Professor:* You switched from 'handsome' to 'beautiful'. Why?

*Director:* Beautiful is a broader idea. I don't want to limit my praise of philosophy.

*Actor:* You're just saying 'beautiful' because it sounds ludicrous to say philosophers are handsome.

*Director:* Handsome is a lesser beauty, true.

*Actor:* Then your idea of 'handsome' is limited to the physical.

*Director:* My idea of beauty is limited to the physical, too.

*Actor:* What? Don't you believe certain ideas are beautiful? Or are you saying ideas are physical?

*Director:* I'm not sure of my footing here. But I'll say yes. Ideas are physical because they exist in the brains of those who hold them.

*Actor:* So you don't believe in transcendent ideas?

*Director:* No, I don't.

*Actor:* But isn't that what philosophy was taken with for thousands of years?

*Director:* What can I say? That may be true. But it doesn't change how I think.

*Professor:* Director is a materialist.

*Actor:* What does that mean?

*Professor:* He thinks the only things that exist are physical, material.

*Actor:* Is that what you think?

*Director:* Again, I think I'm out of my depth.

*Professor:* Oh, he's not out of his depth. Ask him if he believes in ghosts, spirits, things beyond.

*Actor:* Do you?

*Director:* No, I don't.

*Actor:* Then I feel sorry for you.

### 5

*Director:* Why feel sorry for me? I should feel sorry for you.

*Actor:* Why would you feel sorry for me?

*Director:* Because you might not value the physical highly enough.

*Actor:* What physical things don't I value?

*Director:* Acting ability, for one.

*Actor:* Why do you think I don't value that? But acting is more spiritual than physical.

*Director:* How so?

*Actor:* Acting has to do with ideas. You have to be able to absorb them and make them your own.

*Director:* And that's all it takes?

*Actor:* That's all it takes.

*Director:* Do you want me to keep this just between us?

*Actor:* Why would I?

*Director:* I don't want to give away your secret.

*Actor:* Don't worry. The 'secret' is easy to know but hard to do.

*Director:* What does it mean to absorb an idea?

*Actor:* To take it in and understand it in full.

*Director:* Understanding, okay. And to make it your own?

*Actor:* To live the idea.

*Director:* To the exclusion of all other ideas?

*Actor:* Well, there's some controversy here. Some say you need to keep a core of your own. Others say you must surrender even this.

*Director:* What do you do?

*Actor:* I've tried both.

*Director:* And which do you prefer?

*Actor:* It depends on the role.

*Director:* Some are more demanding than others?

*Actor:* Of course.

*Director:* And for the most demanding? What do you do?

*Actor:* I give myself over completely.

*Director:* Are you original when you do this?

*Actor:* I am.

*Director:* What if the role isn't unique?

*Actor:* By giving myself to it I make it unique.

*Director:* What about unique roles? Does that change things?

*Actor:* I'm not sure I follow.

*Director:* If you're given a unique role, one that hasn't been done before, aren't you original no matter how good or bad your performance?

*Actor:* I don't like that idea.

*Director:* Why?

*Actor:* Because it's like infamy versus fame. Anyone can be infamous.

*Director:* Funny you of all people should bring up the idea of fame. Do you know what fame is?

*Actor:* It's being known far and wide.

*Director:* Oh.

*Actor:* What 'oh'?

*Director:* I thought you might say it's being known by many.

*Actor:* That's what being known far and wide means. Being known by many.

*Director:* Yes, but 'many' what?

*Actor:* What are you talking about?

*Director:* Many original souls, or many that are all the same?

*Actor:* I prefer to be known by original souls.

*Director:* How do you reach them?

*Actor:* By being original myself.

*Director:* And for that you're famous.

*Actor:* Yes.

*Professor:* Fame is your way.

*Actor:* No, I wouldn't say that, Professor.

*Professor:* But you're famous.

*Director:* Not all the original want fame. Right, Actor?

*Actor:* It's true. Just look at Professor.

*Professor:* I've achieved a fair amount of fame—among a generation of students, through inspired teaching; among my peers, through articles and books.

*Director:* Yes, but now that you've had a taste of fame—do you want more?

## 6

*Professor:* Why would I? What good would it do? I'm known by those who matter to me.

*Actor:* And you, Director?

*Director:* I'm not sure I'm known.

*Actor:* How so?

*Director:* Well, what would I be known for? What idea?

*Actor:* You're the idea of philosophy.

*Director:* No. So many have said so much about philosophy. There is no one idea. And why do you think that is?

*Actor:* Because so many philosophers have been famous.

*Director:* What do you mean?

*Actor:* People see philosophy as a vehicle for fame. Each path to fame involves a different idea.

*Director:* I'll have to think about that. But is philosophy really a vehicle for fame?

*Actor:* Necessarily? I don't think so.

*Director:* Because you've known philosophers who don't seek fame?

*Actor:* Well, you two are the only philosophers I know.

*Director:* How do you know I'm a philosopher?

*Actor:* You talk about it often enough.

*Director:* Anyone who talks about philosophy is a philosopher?

*Actor:* Of course not.

*Director:* Then what makes a philosopher? What's the idea of philosophy?

*Professor:* Maybe it's the idea of having no idea.

*Actor:* Maybe it is! Director has no idea!

*Director:* Oh, I think I have more ideas than I care to admit. But why does the absence of ideas have to be an idea?

*Actor:* It's an ideal. Something you strive to live up to.

*Director:* Strive to have nothing?

*Actor:* Sure. Don't you know about those monks who strive for exactly that?

*Director:* No, that's not me. That seems a pointless endeavor.

*Actor:* Then what do you strive for?

*Director:* Now you've got me at a loss. What's worth striving for?

*Actor:* Uniqueness.

*Director:* Why?

*Actor:* Because that's the only way to live, to truly live.

*Director:* Those who suffer from sameness don't live?

*Actor:* Don't you agree?

*Director:* I don't know. I can imagine those who are the same saying that those who strive to be unique are all the same. And aren't they?

*Actor:* No! Each striving for uniqueness is unique.

*Director:* Striving is enough? Or do you have to become unique?

*Actor:* Striving is good. But becoming unique is best.

*Director:* But you said striving for uniqueness is unique. That implies striving is as good as achieving the goal.

*Actor:* Look, you never just wake up one morning and say, "I'm unique. I'll strive no more."

*Director:* Do you fail to say that because you know you are in fact unique but know that's not enough?

*Actor:* The journey never ends.

*Director:* I see. And do you know where you're going on this journey?

*Actor:* The journey is filled with wonder and surprise.

*Director:* But you don't know where you're going.

*Actor:* How can you? Where you're going has never been reached.

*Director:* You're blazing a trail?

*Actor:* Yes, exactly.

*Director:* So those who would be the same can follow you?

*Actor:* There will always be those who want to be the same.

*Director:* But what if you don't blaze as you go? What if you leave no path to follow? What if no one but you knows what you've discovered? Has it all been for nothing? Must the fame of your journey be spread?

*Actor:* Director, you're talking about an inhuman isolation. Who wants that? Of course we want to share what we find. Of course we want people to see what we've seen. They can see and then get back to their own way.

*Professor:* Actor makes a good point. You, Director, are playing the radical today.

*Director:* And as radical, am I unique?

*Professor:* As unique as radicals can be.

### 7

*Actor:* That's a failing in Director's eyes.

*Director:* How so?

*Actor:* You don't want to be 'as unique as'. You want to be wholly unique.

*Director:* Do I? How do you know I don't want to be one with other philosophers, not unique at all?

*Professor:* He's uttering the greatest heresy.

*Actor:* What heresy?

*Professor:* That all philosophers say essentially the same thing.

*Actor:* Why is that a heresy?

*Professor:* Because if they say the same thing, then every difference they utter is nonsense.

*Director:* I'm not sure that follows. But so what if philosophers are full of nonsense? What harm comes of that?

*Actor:* People trust philosophers. And if all philosophers speak nonsense, their trust is misplaced.

*Director:* But why would people trust philosophers?

*Actor:* Because they camouflage their nonsense in sense.

*Director:* But why do that? What's the idea?

*Actor:* Maybe all philosophers are jokers.

*Director:* And who gets the joke? Other philosophers?

*Actor:* Why not?

*Director:* But what's the point? Why not just become comedians in the open? Why conceal the humor?

*Professor:* Oh, that's enough of this. Of course philosophers don't all speak the same thing. Haven't you ever been to a philosophy department? I'll tell you about mine. There are bitter arguments among the professors. Their students follow and divide into camps. They, all of them—no doubt—don't say the same thing.

*Actor:* Maybe they're not real philosophers.

*Director:* Professor, what do the professors and students argue about?

*Professor:* Ideas.

*Director:* They want to know whose ideas are better?

*Professor:* Yes.

*Director:* What sort of ideas?

*Professor:* The ones causing the most controversy are those concerning justice.

*Director:* What justice is?

*Professor:* Right.

*Actor:* Justice is getting what you deserve.

*Professor:* Yes, but what do you deserve? And who decides? Those are the questions.

*Director:* And the answers are, or are backed by, ideas.

*Professor:* Naturally.

*Actor:* But then those ideas simply define the conclusions. Here's an example. Justice is for tall people to rule. Therefore tall people should rule. You know you want tall people to rule so you define justice that way.

*Professor:* A true philosopher starts with the question and then arrives at the answer, not the other way round.

*Director:* And this goes for any idea?

*Professor:* Any idea.

*Director:* So all ideas are born of questions?

*Professor:* Without the question there's no idea.

*Actor:* You know, some people would say ideas exist and we simply have to discover them.

*Professor:* That may be. But we discover them through questions.

*Director:* But, practically speaking, there can be no idea without a corresponding question?

*Professor:* Correct.

*Director:* If we ask questions about ideas, what will we get?

*Professor:* An idea about ideas.

*Actor:* What good will that do us?

*Professor:* I really don't know.

### 8

*Actor:* So you're disinterested when it comes to questioning ideas? You don't know what you want the questioning to bring?

*Professor:* Of course. That's the only way to get at truth.

*Director:* How do we begin?

*Professor:* Let's say you cherish a certain idea. Wouldn't you wonder how you got it?

*Actor:* Not really. Who can say where an idea comes from? The point is that you have it.

*Director:* I'd like to know where I got it from.

*Actor:* Why would it matter?

*Director:* I'd like to know who to blame.

*Actor:* Be serious.

*Director:* But I am.

*Actor:* So let's say you got it from someone else. What would you do?

*Director:* I'd confront them. 'You gave me an idea. Explain yourself.'

*Actor:* And if the idea you took from them wasn't the one they intended?

*Director:* Then maybe I'm to blame.

*Professor:* All this is fine until we come to cherished ideas. No one likes to talk about them.

*Director:* And that's a mistake.

*Actor:* I don't know, Director. Sometimes we need an idea to comfort us, to nurture us. Opening it up to scrutiny by others can take those things away.

*Director:* Because we'll realize the idea is false?

*Actor:* Well, that's an interesting point. Can an idea be false?

*Director:* Can a hope be false?

*Actor:* Yes.

*Director:* Can ideas give us hope?

*Actor:* They can.

*Director:* Then ideas can be false.

*Actor:* I'm not so sure about that logic, but I take the point.

*Director:* Can scrutiny indicate when hope is false?

*Actor:* It can.

*Director:* So scrutiny is good, is to be welcomed.

*Actor:* I don't know.

*Professor:* You're worried scrutiny is uncomfortable?

*Actor:* Who likes to be uncomfortable?

*Professor:* Sometimes those who seek truth.

*Actor:* Truth can be overrated.

*Director:* That's quite an idea. Where did you get it?

*Actor:* I came to it on my own.

*Director:* Does it comfort you?

*Actor:* Yes, it does.

*Director:* It tells you you don't have to strive?

*Actor:* It tells me to be honest, but not brutally honest.

*Director:* With yourself?

*Actor:* And others. You have to seek truth, but not too much.

*Director:* Why not?

*Actor:* You can wear yourself out.

*Director:* The truths you seek, why do you seek them?

*Actor:* Because they'll help me in my life.

*Director:* Help you steer, or something like that?

*Actor:* Yes, exactly like that. And you know that's important and good.

*Director:* I would steer by truth. And you, Professor?

*Professor:* Of course. But I think we have a war problem again.

*Actor:* What do you mean?

*Professor:* Our side has truths; the enemy has truths. If we learn an enemy truth, do we steer by that truth?

*Actor:* We do—in order to do them harm.

*Professor:* And what of those of the enemy who don't abide by that truth? What if there are those who abide by our truth?

*Actor:* There can't be many of them or the enemy wouldn't be our enemy. But I'm afraid it's bad luck for them.

*Professor:* How so?

*Actor:* Their atmosphere is toxic to their truth.

*Director:* What can be done for them?

*Actor:* We have to win the war quickly—and they have to learn to resist.

*Professor:* We should always resist when our ideas are unpopular.

*Actor:* Unpopular? They're more than that.

*Director:* What are they?

*Actor:* Hated.

### 9

*Director:* What can they do about the hate?

*Actor:* They can attack the ideas that support it.

*Director:* Hate needs support?

*Actor:* Of course it does.

*Director:* So those who hate are thinkers?

*Actor:* No, not thinkers. They hold their ideas unthinkingly.

*Professor:* But then why attack the supporting ideas?

*Actor:* We're hoping the haters will, unthinkingly, take up better ideas.

*Director:* Ones less supportive of hate.

*Actor:* Right.

*Director:* What do you think, Professor?

*Professor:* I think we need to make them think.

*Actor:* But you can't force people to think.

*Professor:* I'm not talking about forcing. I'm talking about persuading.

*Director:* Are haters open to persuasion?

*Professor:* As a rule? No. But there are exceptions. And we should concentrate there.

*Actor:* Yes, but encouragement to think feels like an attack to those who don't think.

*Director:* Even more reason to know the signs.

*Actor:* What signs?

*Director:* The signs of those who are impervious to reason.

*Actor:* Yes, we can't bother with them. But how do we know they're impervious?

*Director:* With some it's obvious. With others we have to probe.

*Actor:* Probe in a way that's not perceived as attack.

*Director:* Yes.

*Professor:* Books can help in this.

*Actor:* How?

*Professor:* If you can get the non-thinkers to read, the book might challenge their ideas. At worst they dislike the book.

*Actor:* And its author.

*Professor:* True.

*Actor:* But do books really address the unthinking?

*Director:* I've read a few of your books, Professor. They're hardly for the unlearned.

*Professor:* There's lack of thought among the learned, too.

*Actor:* Then that's your battle—a battle among the elite.

*Director:* But what do you mean by elite? Higher education is increasingly common.

*Actor:* The elite are those with money, those who occupy positions of power.

*Professor:* You think they read my books?

*Actor:* If not, then how do you achieve change?

*Professor:* Real change happens when a thinker, at any level, reads my book and thinks a new thought, or is encouraged in one long held.

*Actor:* Director?

*Director:* Professor, what was your last book about?

*Professor:* The philosophical import of the words 'and' and 'but'.

*Director:* And that seems important to me. But how many among the elite—busy executives, say—would have time for this?

*Actor:* So the ideas we present have to fit someone's schedule?

*Director:* Either that or we persuade them to make time for us.

*Actor:* How can we do that?

*Director:* We pique their interest.

*Actor:* Yes, but how?

*Director:* How do you pique your audience's interest?

*Actor:* I talk about things they care about.

*Director:* Well, what does a busy executive care about?

*Actor:* Who knows? Stock price? Quarterly earnings?

*Director:* Sure. So maybe we question the idea behind price. What is that idea?

*Actor:* That the market is the best means to value the worth of a company. But executives don't want to question that.

*Director:* Why not?

*Actor:* What good would questioning do?

*Professor:* Maybe they'll find a better way to value. One that puts less stress on them. The new idea might be in their interest.

*Director:* So in questioning one idea we make way for another.

*Professor:* A better idea.

*Director:* But we don't know what that better idea is.

*Professor:* No, we don't. But we're clearing the way.

*Director:* And if questioning an idea is enough to bring it down, it's time to bring it down.

*Actor:* I agree with that.

*Director:* So we should question all ideas, and see which ones stand and which ones fall?

*Actor:* Yes. And do everyone a service.

10

*Professor:* Yes, but there are ideas that are so strong we don't even know they're ideas. What of them?

*Actor:* It's not time for them to fall.

*Professor:* Even if they're bad ideas?

*Actor:* Can bad ideas be strong?

*Professor:* Are you really asking that? Isn't it more surprising when good ideas are strong?

*Director:* So what do we do with strong bad ideas?

*Professor:* We have to be careful. Questioning them can bring ruin.

*Actor:* What's an example?

*Professor:* An executive stands up and says, 'I've been questioning my company's stock. I don't think it reflects the state of the firm. It's valued much too highly, perhaps by half. Here, let me show you why.'

*Director:* That would likely bring trouble. But is that the best example we can find?

*Actor:* I think it's a good example. The executive basically says, 'I'm no longer playing the game we play.' That's what any good question says.

*Director:* Is there a way to say that without the trouble?

*Actor:* I suppose you can say it from outside. What trouble will I, for instance, get into if I challenge someone's stock?

*Director:* But if you're outside, do you really know best what needs questioning? Think of acting. I don't know what needs questioning there. But you likely do.

*Actor:* Yes, and I have something I'd like to question. Realism.

*Professor:* I don't understand.

*Actor:* Realism, especially in historical fiction, is usually a joke.

*Director:* Can you say more?

*Actor:* Actors try to be realistic in their portrayal of people from times gone by. But how can they be? We know so little of the past.

*Professor:* So what should they do? Be unrealistic?

*Actor:* Why not? It amounts to much the same thing. In fact, unrealism might be liberating, freeing us up to think new thoughts about the past.

*Director:* Would you get in trouble for questioning this way?

*Actor:* If I were chosen for a part in a historical drama? Yes, I would—unless I found the right director.

*Professor:* And the right producers, and the right investors.

*Actor:* True.

*Director:* But this has been done before. I'm not sure it's as radical an idea as it seems.

*Professor:* What would be a radical idea?

*Director:* Something that challenges the unchallenged—bad ideas so strong that we don't even see them.

*Actor:* Bad ideas among the basic assumptions in our lives? But we do challenge these 'unchallenged' ideas. Think of politics. Each side thinks the other side has bad ideas. And these ideas are strong among a sizable portion of the population.

*Director:* But they're not strong enough. We're talking about ideas so strong the political process never touches them.

*Actor:* Ideas that undergird that process?

*Director:* Yes.

*Professor:* Oh, but you've never been to my school. People question the basic political process all the time.

*Actor:* But what don't they question? That's what we're looking for. Do they question the value of your school?

*Professor:* They do. And they even question the value of questioning.

*Actor:* Is there nothing left to question? Director?

*Director:* There must be something to question.

*Actor:* Then name it.

*Director:* We can question the idea of language.

*Actor:* What does that mean?

*Director:* What do we think language does?

*Actor:* It communicates.

*Director:* Communicates what?

*Actor:* Ideas.

*Director:* Is the idea in my mind always the same as it is in your mind after I communicate it to you?

*Actor:* Not always, no.

*Director:* So language doesn't always do what we think it does.

*Actor:* It doesn't, and that's a good point.

*Director:* What good does this point do us?

*Actor:* It teaches us not to put too much emphasis on words.

*Professor:* Yes, yes. This is an old argument. People raise it in my school.

*Actor:* I know who doesn't put too much emphasis on words.

*Director:* Who?

*Actor:* Those impervious to reason.

## 11

*Director:* But let's say we're dealing with the reasonable, and we're questioning all sorts of things. I think we have to ask—is our questioning meeting with success?

*Actor:* You mean, is it bringing down bad ideas.

*Professor:* These things take time, Director—especially from the outside, as you know.

*Actor:* How much time?

*Professor:* A generation, usually, at least.

*Actor:* But how long has the radical questioning been going on?

*Professor:* In this country? Long enough to see some real improvements.

*Actor:* And this is political questioning?

*Professor:* In effect? Of course it is. Politics is how things change.

*Actor:* But what if people don't want things to change? What if they're conservative?

*Professor:* Conservatives can question. They like to question the progressive.

*Actor:* So what happens with politics? The strongest idea wins? Conservative or progressive?

*Professor:* Yes, generally speaking.

*Actor:* But then the strength of an idea depends on numbers, votes. We all know that's not true.

*Professor:* Not all of us know that. But I agree with you, on one condition. We should say the political strength—the political strength—of an idea, in this country, depends on votes.

*Actor:* An idea can be strong but not have political strength?

*Professor:* Yes, absolutely.

*Actor:* And an idea can have political strength but not be good.

*Professor:* Correct.

*Actor:* We're back at our question about what makes an idea good.

*Professor:* An idea is good when it brings on the flourishing of human life.

*Actor:* Yes, but which humans?

*Director:* And what does it mean to flourish?

*Professor:* A human flourishes when it's prosperous and happy.

*Actor:* Why not just happy?

*Professor:* Asks the multimillionaire.

*Actor:* Don't hold my wealth against me. And I won't hold your tenure at a highly prestigious school against you.

*Director:* You know, Professor makes the least money of the three of us.

*Actor:* How do you know that? Did you ask him how much he makes?

*Director:* Yes.

*Professor:* But I didn't take offense. If you don't ask questions you're at risk of becoming one of the thoughtless. You'll have nothing to think about.

*Actor:* I'll think about ideas. I'll gnaw on them like a worm. How's that?

*Director:* He pretends he doesn't know what all his peers are making on their films. And if they make more, it gnaws at him like a worm.

*Actor:* All this talk of gnawing is making me hungry again! But I know the truth. You can't live on ideas.

*Professor:* Tell us why not.

*Actor:* Let's assume that when you feed on ideas you come to know certain things.

*Professor:* That's a fair assumption.

*Actor:* Yes. But at some point you know enough.

*Director:* So you stop chewing? Be careful not to swallow your ideas whole.

*Actor:* Thank you for the good advice. But my point is that when you know enough, you need to take action.

*Professor:* You think action requires the stoppage of thought? That's a blasphemy, Actor.

*Actor:* Blasphemy against what?

*Professor:* Reason.

*Director:* Oh, he's teasing you, Actor. Reason isn't holy. We can reason about reason.

*Actor:* But then we never get beyond reason.

*Professor:* Is that so bad? Everything is subject to reason, including reason. Nothing goes beyond. There's a kind of comfort in that. Wouldn't you agree?

*Actor:* I'm not so sure. Haven't you heard of analysis paralysis?

*Professor:* Of course I have. That happens when you use reason as an excuse not to act. But we can act and reason as we do.

*Actor:* So there's never a time when we should stop reasoning?

*Professor:* There's always something to reason on. The world is filled to the brim with ideas.

*Actor:* Some places are idea impoverished. Not every place is like your campus.

*Professor:* We have many colorful ideas, yes. But places with a grim, single idea can be filled to full with it. There's no such thing as a vacuum of ideas. When one idea goes, another rushes in.

*Actor:* Always?

*Professor:* Always.

### 12

*Actor:* What about artificial intelligences? Will they always have ideas?

*Professor:* I think they will. Without ideas, what would they do? What would they be?

*Actor:* I don't know. But computers today don't have ideas.

*Professor:* They have the ideas of their makers. Artificial intelligences differ in that they might modify those ideas.

*Actor:* But not the most basic idea?

*Director:* What idea is that?

*Actor:* The idea of life.

*Professor:* Their life?

*Actor:* And ours. What it means to live. That's a question now, you know.

*Professor:* It's been a question for a very long time. But maybe they'll show us the way when it comes to this.

*Actor:* I think artificial intelligences should question all ideas, including our idea of life. I'd love to see where it all ends up.

*Professor:* Maybe they would end up as philosophers.

*Director:* There's more to philosophy than questioning.

*Professor:* Yes, of course. But maybe we could give these intelligences that something more?

*Director:* I don't know.

*Actor:* Why not?

*Director:* It has to do with love.

*Professor:* Can intelligence love? Or is love a matter of the heart?

*Actor:* That's the real question here. Can an artificial intelligence have a heart? Can it be attracted to a beautiful server rack in a data center somewhere in the middle of nowhere?

*Director:* I don't see why not. After all, the intelligence has ideas. And love, love is an idea.

*Actor:* So we should question love?

*Professor:* Vigorously. So much in the world goes wrong because of love.

*Actor:* You two are teasing now. So, what, if we want to sabotage an artificial intelligence, we give it the idea of love?

*Professor:* This is no joking matter. What happens with an artificial intelligence driven mad from love? It could be catastrophic, depending what it controls.

*Director:* But this is an old tale. The tyrant falls in love and love brings him low.

*Actor:* Why do you say 'him'? There are female tyrants, you know.

*Professor:* Of course there are. And love can bring them low, too. No one is immune.

*Actor:* Because we can't help what we feel.

*Director:* Yes, but why do we feel what we feel?

*Actor:* What do you mean? We just feel it.

*Professor:* I know what he means. What goes into feeling other than thought? The ideas we hold shape our feelings.

*Actor:* Oh, I don't believe it. And here's an example. If I cherish the idea that I shouldn't fall in love with short people, I can still fall in love with a short person. Love, the feeling of love, overturns every idea.

*Professor:* Not necessarily. Someone can cling so desperately to an idea that love has no chance.

*Actor:* But how do we know that's what's happening?

*Professor:* Because they're miserable.

*Actor:* Why cling to an idea that makes you miserable?

*Professor:* Because without it your compass is smashed. And, obviously, I'm not talking about your example of tall or short. We take our bearings in this world by the ideas we hold.

*Actor:* That's a luxury.

*Director:* What do you mean?

*Actor:* The 'we' Professor speaks of is by and large the elite.

*Director:* How so?

*Actor:* Most of us take our bearing by facts, often times brutal facts.

*Professor:* Ideas are how we interpret the facts.

*Actor:* You don't think we have direct access to the facts?

*Professor:* No, I don't.

*Actor:* You're more of a professor than I thought!

*Director:* What does that mean?

*Actor:* He's not aware of the real facts of life.

*Professor:* Awareness is an idea, you know.

*Actor:* So is breathing. And yet we don't have to think in order to breathe.

*Professor:* Yes, but with awareness there's thinking you're aware and then there's being aware.

*Director:* How can we distinguish between the two? I mean, if I know today is Wednesday, and you don't—I'm aware and you're not? It's that simple?

*Professor:* It's that simple, yes. But what if I know that the idea of 'Wednesday' is relatively new in human history, and you don't—who's aware then?

*Actor:* Everything is 'relatively new' in human history. Our history keeps changing.

*Director:* Then in order to be aware we need to be current in our history?

*Actor:* Awareness can have to do with ancient things, sure. But the awareness that counts is the awareness of oneself and one's surroundings.

*Director:* How do we know if we're aware that way?

*Actor:* We're able to navigate our surroundings.

*Director:* So awareness is a matter of success? We successfully navigate ourselves around our surroundings?

*Actor:* That's right.

*Director:* But can't someone who's aware have bad luck? Or are you one who believes we can overcome luck? That's a modern belief.

*Actor:* Well, maybe I'm post-modern here. Luck overcomes all.

*Director:* Even your skill as an actor?

*Actor:* I might act in a movie, and act very well. But the movie might still be very poorly received.

*Director:* Why?

*Actor:* It might not go with the spirit of the times.

*Director:* Fifty years earlier, or fifty years later, and it might have been a great success?

*Actor:* Precisely.

*Professor:* Then you weren't aware of the times. Otherwise, you wouldn't have taken the part. It wasn't luck. It was your failure to know.

### 13

*Director:* What's the idea of luck?

*Actor:* That things happen beyond our control; that they don't happen because of what we do or don't do.

*Director:* So luck is liberating?

*Actor:* In a way, yes. But luck also tyrannizes over us.

*Director:* That's an odd combination—liberty, tyranny. What's the opposite of luck?

*Actor:* Control, I guess. Control over our fate.

*Director:* Is control liberating?

*Actor:* It liberates us from luck, from chance—at least to some small degree.

*Director:* But can control tyrannize?

*Actor:* The desire for too much control tyrannizes over the soul.

*Director:* So we have that odd combination again—liberty, tyranny.

*Actor:* The way out is through the mean.

*Director:* Some control and some luck?

*Actor:* Exactly.

*Director:* What would you say is the idea behind that?

*Actor:* Moderation in all things.

*Professor:* But then we're not moderate in our moderation.

*Actor:* True.

*Director:* What would it mean to be moderate in moderation?

*Professor:* To take one or more things to the extreme.

*Director:* What should we take to the extreme?

*Professor:* I'm not sure there's any one recommendation that suits all.

*Director:* What are you immoderate in?

*Professor:* Learning. And I teach my students to be immoderate here, as well.

*Actor:* What's the idea behind learning?

*Professor:* That learning makes you better.

*Director:* Makes you feel better? Or makes you somehow objectively better?

*Professor:* Both.

*Director:* Then why would anyone not learn all they can?

*Professor:* It takes effort.

*Actor:* It takes a great deal of effort for me to learn a new part.

*Director:* Yes, but not all learning takes effort. I can learn about a newly discovered star, for instance, just by reading the news.

*Professor:* Knowledge worth having isn't often in the news. That's when it's hard to learn.

*Director:* You mean you have to piece things together on your own.

*Professor:* Precisely. And that's difficult.

*Actor:* So you want your students to be immoderate in difficult learning. But won't that wear them out? Don't they need rest?

*Professor:* Of course they do. But they rest only as long as they need. Then they get back to work.

*Director:* That sounds like a moderate plan to me.

*Actor:* And what comes of moderate plans?

*Director:* I suppose it's health.

*Actor:* You can never have too much health.

*Professor:* But you can. Sometimes a little sickness goes a long way. It can help you discover things you otherwise wouldn't see.

*Director:* Because of the perspective it affords?

*Professor:* Yes.

*Actor:* So it's health in moderation, for the sake of discovery? I'm not sure I like that, but let's say it's so. Still, I'd like to find the thing that trumps moderation.

*Director:* That thing is philosophy.

*Actor:* Is philosophy what we're doing here today?

*Director:* Well, we're having breakfast and coffee here today. But yes, we're also philosophizing a bit.

*Actor:* Why is philosophy beyond moderation?

*Director:* Because moderation alone can't tell us why moderation is good. Something beyond moderation must say.

*Actor:* And philosophy provides that critical point of view?

*Director:* It does.

### 14

*Actor:* Then is critical inquiry the most important idea? That's what philosophy is, right?

*Director:* That's part of philosophy, yes. But there are two types of inquiry. The first is when we inquire alone; the second is when we inquire with others.

*Actor:* Why are they different?

*Director:* Each type has its merits and failings.

*Actor:* What's the merit of inquiring alone?

*Director:* We can concentrate without distractions.

*Actor:* And the failing?

*Director:* We might not think of everything that should be considered.

*Actor:* Then I take it the merits and failings of inquiry with others are the reverse.

*Director:* Yes, we prod each other to think comprehensively; but we distract each other's train of thought.

*Professor:* Distraction can be a virtue. Sometimes we build up so much momentum heading in one direction that we aren't even thinking any more. We just roll along, even when we're headed the wrong way. It can be good to be forced to stop.

*Actor:* How can you force someone to stop?

*Professor:* You have to be blunt with them.

*Actor:* That assumes you know the truth about their way.

*Professor:* No, I can tell someone they're wrong without knowing what's right. To put it perhaps too simply, I might know that the square root of one million isn't one, without knowing what it actually is. If you say it's one, I say you're wrong.

*Actor:* Yes, but you knew the truth, the truth that the answer isn't one.

*Director:* I agree. And the point is important—because philosophy knows lots of negative truths.

*Professor:* That's what makes it obnoxious to some.

*Actor:* Does philosophy know positive truth?

*Director:* It does. But it's always willing to put that truth to the test.

*Actor:* That's how philosophy is extreme. An extreme willingness. But how does philosophy put itself to the test? Is there a critical faculty beyond philosophy?

*Professor:* It comes down to how we feel.

*Actor:* What do you mean?

*Professor:* We judge philosophy by how it makes us feel. That's the 'faculty' beyond philosophy.

*Actor:* Some people feel good about philosophy and some feel bad? And there's nothing higher than or beyond this feeling?

*Professor:* Nothing at all.

*Actor:* Director, is that true? Are you a philosopher because philosophy feels good?

*Director:* It doesn't always feel good. But basically? Yes, it feels good.

*Actor:* Is it an acquired taste? Or is it natural to some?

*Director:* I'm inclined to say it's acquired. But some seem to acquire the taste so early that it seems natural to them.

*Actor:* So is there a hierarchy of philosophers based on how early they came to philosophy?

*Professor:* No, it doesn't work like that. You can come to something early and make little of it. And those who come late often make up for lost time with zeal.

*Director:* Do you want to come to philosophy, Actor?

*Actor:* Who says I haven't? I use the negative method in my work.

*Director:* The negative method?

*Actor:* I study what a character is not. Then I allow myself to be what the character is.

*Director:* Without knowing what the character is?

*Actor:* Yes. And that's life giving. It allows the character freedom, the freedom to breathe. People don't know what they are. At best they know what they're not. My art reflects life.

*Professor:* But people feel a need to know what they are.

*Actor:* Then they should follow my method and see what appears when the negatives are known. They might not be able to pin their identity down. But they'll live it nonetheless.

### 15

*Professor:* Are you saying we don't need to know ourselves in order to live as we should?

*Actor:* We should know what we're not.

*Professor:* What's wrong with knowing what you are?

*Actor:* It fences you in. It limits you.

*Professor:* Fences make good neighbors. Limits keep you sane.

*Actor:* And if those are your highest goals in life, more power to you.

*Director:* What's your highest goal, Actor?

*Actor:* Excellence.

*Director:* Even at the cost of making enemies and going insane?

*Actor:* Oh, lack of limits doesn't make you insane. It makes you a little mad—in a creative, positive way. As for enemies? Those with no enemies have no friends.

*Professor:* Creativity very much comes from having limits—just limits not had by most. You have limits in your work, Actor. You limit yourself to the negative.

*Actor:* True, but you agree about enemies?

*Professor:* I don't. While you can't be everyone's friend, you can remain neutral to many and have a few friends.

*Director:* Actor, why do you think enemies come with friends?

*Actor:* Because friends share something good. And there are always enemies to the good.

*Director:* Why?

*Actor:* Jealousy.

*Director:* It's really that simple?

*Actor:* It's really that simple.

*Director:* Can you say more about the good in question?

*Actor:* It's trust, and mutual respect, and pleasure in one another's company. Not everyone can have these things.

*Director:* Why not?

*Actor:* They haven't prepared themselves for it.

*Director:* Prepared?

*Actor:* Through discipline.

*Director:* Ah. But what is this discipline?

*Actor:* You can't trust another unless you trust yourself.

*Director:* And trusting yourself takes discipline?

*Actor:* Of course.

*Director:* Why?

*Actor:* Because if you're not disciplined there's nothing to trust—no consistency, no reliability.

*Director:* What about mutual respect?

*Actor:* You can't respect another unless you respect yourself.

*Director:* And that takes discipline?

*Actor:* Your discipline is what you respect.

*Director:* What about taking pleasure in one another's company?

*Actor:* You can't take pleasure in another unless you can take pleasure in yourself.

*Director:* Okay, but that requires discipline?

*Actor:* Yes. You can't overindulge in yourself.

*Director:* Really? What happens if you do?

*Actor:* You grow weak.

*Director:* And it takes strength in order to enjoy another?

*Actor:* Of course it does.

*Director:* But what if I'm sick and weak, and a good friend comes to visit me? Can't I take pleasure in the visit?

*Actor:* Yes, but you'll be using whatever strength you have.

*Director:* So discipline is key—don't deplete your strength. Marshall it wisely.

*Actor:* Right.

*Director:* And if you have no discipline, you're jealous of those who have it.

*Actor:* Naturally.

*Director:* And we can't be friends with those who are jealous of us.

*Actor:* You might think you're friends, but you're not.

*Director:* Well, Professor, what do you think of all this?

*Professor:* I think discipline is always for the sake of something else. Discipline is a subordinate idea. When it takes the primary place, something is wrong.

*Actor:* Not too many are disciplined for discipline's sake. I think the real problem is when the 'something else' is bad.

*Director:* Disciplined for something bad. Hmm, yes. Or can we say disciplined for something undesirable?

*Actor:* Sure we can. But what's an example?

*Director:* You're disciplined in your work for the sake of being able to gloat over your peers.

*Actor:* Gloating is undesirable, yes. But what's another example?

*Director:* You're disciplined in what you say to others because you're afraid of seeming a fool.

*Actor:* Too many of us are afraid of seeming a fool. Sometimes seeming a fool is the only way to move things forward. What's another example?

*Director:* You're disciplined in what you say because you don't want to be obnoxious.

*Actor:* Philosophy's curse. So let me ask. Is philosophy disciplined?

## 16

*Professor:* Philosophy is disciplined in its use of logic.

*Director:* Are you saying the logic is strict?

*Professor:* Sometimes philosophers use less than strict logic—but they're disciplined when they do.

*Actor:* What's less than strict? False?

*Professor:* Not necessarily. I think of less than strict as allowing room to breathe.

*Actor:* You don't feel trapped by the logic.

*Professor:* Correct.

*Actor:* But aren't there times when we want to trap someone with logic?

*Professor:* What, like a liar?

*Actor:* Sure.

*Professor:* That may be. Then the logic must be strict. Or it can start out loose and then become strict. But logic is only as good as its premises.

*Actor:* True, but why do you bring that up?

*Professor:* What if society accepts as true a premise that's false? The premise that everyone lies all the time, for instance.

*Actor:* What if?

*Professor:* How do we challenge the premise?

*Actor:* We show that not everyone lies all the time.

*Director:* But what if they do?

*Actor:* Then we take a longer road. We start by establishing the premise that lying is bad. Then, over time, fewer people might lie, thinking it's bad—which would go to prove that the first premise, that everyone lies all the time, is false.

*Director:* How many untrue premises do you think are out there?

*Actor:* Countless. And they're accepted as true.

*Director:* So logic might seem strict and sound, but be false?

*Actor:* Of course.

*Professor:* Loose logic concedes that it might be mistaken. It's open to correction. Strict logic isn't usually open like this. It believes its premises are absolutely true, and that all the inferences it draws from them are absolutely true. So there's no room to breathe if you're someone who sees untruth in all this.

*Actor:* So what can we do if the logic is flawed?

*Professor:* Attack the premises or inferences.

*Director:* All this sounds very good. But what do we do when we, as philosophers, know to a certainty that our premises are true, and that we draw the true conclusions from them? Do we accuse ourselves of being too strict? Should we loosen up?

*Professor:* You raise an interesting question about knowledge. Can we ever know to a certainty?

*Actor:* Of course we can. We know that if you jump off a very high bridge, you'll die. There are many certainties like this in life. We know you can't fly off into space by wishing. We know you were born and that you will age and die.

*Professor:* I see you like the 'die' examples. But what if in the distant future we're able to survive a jump from on high? What if we can in fact fly off into space? What if we're never born and never die?

*Actor:* Yes, yes. Science fiction. But what matters in reasoning is what's possible now.

*Professor:* How do we know what's possible? What's the idea of the possible?

*Actor:* The possible is something that can be done.

*Professor:* And what role does imagination play in this?

*Actor:* Imagination sometimes shows us the way.

*Professor:* The way to defy the odds, for instance?

*Actor:* For instance, sure. And the way to overcome the hardships those odds impose.

*Professor:* You use imagination in your work.

*Actor:* Of course I do. And I inspire people to do what's possible. There's deep satisfaction in that.

*Professor:* You change the logic.

*Actor:* I change the premise from X is impossible to X is possible.

*Director:* Does that make you enemies?

*Actor:* It certainly does.

*Director:* Some people want X to be impossible.

*Actor:* Absolutely.

*Director:* Why?

*Actor:* They think it's in their interest.

*Director:* Is it in their interest?

*Actor:* It might be. But it doesn't matter. If someone is suffering because X seems impossible, that someone needs to act and prove that X is possible.

*Director:* Prove that its possibility is not just an act put on by you.

*Actor:* Right.

*Director:* But what if it is just an act put on by you?

*Actor:* You mean it's really not possible? I would never act such a part.

*Director:* But how do you know you wouldn't?

*Actor:* What do you mean?

*Director:* You might think it's possible when it's not.

*Actor:* Oh, but you might be surprised. A good script that's acted well can persuade many people to believe something is possible when they hadn't before.

*Director:* Does their belief make the impossible possible?

*Actor:* Don't underestimate the power of belief.

*Director:* Because all that belief puts pressure on those who want X to remain impossible?

*Actor:* It certainly does.

*Director:* And with enough pressure they eventually give in?

*Actor:* Yes. Though not without a fight.

### 17

*Professor:* So you're inciting people to riot?

*Actor:* No, Professor. I'm inciting them to stand up for their beliefs.

*Professor:* For an idea.

*Actor:* Yes, the idea that X is possible.

*Professor:* And this belief will be called X-ism, or something like that?

*Actor:* Who cares what it's called so long as it triumphs?

*Director:* Because the more that's possible the better?

*Actor:* Don't you believe in limitless possibilities?

*Director:* I'm not sure.

*Professor:* Well, I don't. As I've said, I think limits are important.

*Actor:* But how do you know which limits to maintain?

*Professor:* I maintain those that are in my interest.

*Actor:* Name such a limit.

*Professor:* It's in my interest not to name them.

*Actor:* Of course. Director, can you think of any?

*Director:* I think Professor likes to limit his students.

*Professor:* How?

*Director:* By giving them grades.

*Professor:* My course is pass/fail.

*Director:* Then you like to have them fear the fail. That's a limit, isn't it?

*Professor:* It certainly is. And you're right. But I use this limit to the advantage of all. Fear makes them try harder. And the harder they try, the more everyone learns—including me.

*Actor:* You have reasons for your limits.

*Professor:* Of course I do.

*Actor:* But you're imposing limits on your students' thoughts. Anything that doesn't go well with you, goes poorly for their passing.

*Professor:* All I ask is that they have the courage of their ideas. If they do, they pass.

*Actor:* What does that mean, 'courage of their ideas'?

*Professor:* Two things. One, to voice the idea—in class or an essay. Two, to follow the idea—through all it implies.

*Actor:* And you, as teacher, will help them see what it implies.

*Professor:* Yes, but sometimes they help me. And that's a wonderful thing.

*Director:* Is what an idea implies what makes it good or bad? In other words, an idea that implies nothing is neither good nor bad?

*Professor:* I think that's fair to say.

*Actor:* But what idea implies nothing?

*Professor:* The idea of nothing.

*Actor:* That's the belief that nothing is?

*Professor:* That nothingness exists; that there is nothingness in the universe.

*Actor:* But surely that implies... something.

*Professor:* I'm at a loss to say what that something is.

### 18

*Director:* Maybe we should back our way into the idea.

*Actor:* What do you mean?

*Director:* Haven't you ever heard someone say, "It's all been for nothing"?

*Actor:* Of course. You yourself said it today.

*Director:* What does that saying imply?

*Actor:* That no good will ever come of the effort.

*Director:* That view precludes the view that something good always comes of effort.

*Actor:* True.

*Director:* If the effort comes to nothing, is anyone harmed?

*Actor:* It's funny you ask. Haven't you heard the saying 'a little hard work never hurt anyone'?

*Director:* I have. But hard work that comes to nothing might be a disappointment. And doesn't that hurt?

*Professor:* Yes, but disappointment can be a help. It can help us see more clearly.

*Actor:* See why the work was for nothing?

*Professor:* Yes. And next time, the work might be for something.

*Director:* Something good or something bad?

*Actor:* Something good, of course.

*Director:* Work can't be for something bad?

*Actor:* Oh, I suppose it can. But I think people would include 'bad' in 'nothing'.

*Director:* Good is something while bad is nothing? If bad is nothing, who cares if there's bad?

*Professor:* Bad is something, no doubt. A something very different than good.

*Director:* If good and bad are something, what is nothing?

*Actor:* The neutral?

*Professor:* No, the neutral is something. It's a neutral thing. Anything that's a thing can't be nothing. Nothing is, precisely—no thing.

*Director:* Well, I'm glad we've got that all cleared up.

*Professor:* But it's not yet clear. Nothing can't even be a vacuum, a void. A void is a thing.

*Director:* We can't even ascribe adjectives to nothing, can we? There's no big nothing. No little nothing. And so on.

*Professor:* I'm glad you understand. All we can do is stand in awe.

*Actor:* Why would we when we don't know what nothing is?

*Professor:* Nothing is the idea of what we can't know.

*Actor:* What are you saying? Let's look at an example. We can't know how others truly feel. We can understand that someone is, for instance, anxious. But we can't know, can't truly know, just how that feels for them. Are you saying that not knowing is nothing?

*Professor:* Yes, and it's also nothing if we believe we know when we don't.

*Actor:* But what about the harm that comes of such belief? That's not nothing.

*Professor:* True. When we steer by belief we often come to harm.

*Actor:* When we steer by false belief, you mean.

*Professor:* It's best to steer by knowledge. Knowledge is always true. Belief can be true or false. Why take the chance?

*Director:* Yes, but I want to talk about war again. Do we want the enemy to believe the false? Does their false belief bring us good?

*Actor:* What are you saying? Philosophers never engage in war?

*Professor:* Why wouldn't they?

*Actor:* Philosophy seeks to replace belief with knowledge. Philosophers don't distinguish between friend and foe when it comes to this.

*Professor:* I wouldn't be so sure. Consider this. There are those who oppose philosophy. There's little chance they'll ever come around to support it. Philosophers must do them harm or be harmed themselves. Those who oppose us are the enemy. There is no neutral here.

## 19

*Actor:* And they harm them by encouraging false belief? Director?

*Director:* There are two selves to those with false belief—the self that believes, and the self capable of knowledge. A philosopher feeds the self that can know.

*Actor:* So philosophers never encourage false belief.

*Director:* Not if they can help it.

*Professor:* Director, tell us how a philosopher starves the believing self.

*Director:* Starves? Philosophers encourage the true.

*Professor:* And in war?

*Director:* In war a philosopher fights by means other than belief.

*Actor:* You really wouldn't get the enemy to think the false?

*Director:* They already think the false.

*Actor:* What do they think?

*Director:* They believe harming us and our friends is good.

*Actor:* But we all know that's bad.

*Professor:* So is it like this? They believe one plus one is three, so to speak. And they perceive this as good. And they carry on with that bad math and make all sorts of mistakes.

*Director:* Yes, and if they come to see the answer is two—if they see the truth— they see it does no good to do us harm.

*Actor:* That sounds nice. But what if it does do good? I mean, opposing sides have different interests. And they fight for those interests.

*Professor:* And those interests are generally proclaimed in big ideas.

*Actor:* Then we attack the ideas.

*Director:* We attack them with the true math, so to speak?

*Actor:* Absolutely. But how does this play outside of war?

*Director:* What's outside of war?

*Professor:* Character, soul.

*Director:* Ah. Well, whatever is outside, I think the answer is the same. Our math must be true.

*Actor:* But there is no true and accurate math when it comes to character or soul. At best we estimate.

*Director:* And if someone estimates another's character as two plus two equals twenty?

*Actor:* We know that's too high.

*Director:* Do we encourage them to come down?

*Actor:* Yes.

*Director:* And when they do? When they come down to eight, for instance?

*Actor:* They'll feel better the closer they get to the truth.

*Director:* They may even find it?

*Actor:* Yes, but it's a moving target. Character, soul—it's not static. It can't be measured once and for all.

*Director:* So rather than math, this is more a matter of feeling? We feel our way to this truth?

*Actor:* For these things we do, yes.

*Professor:* We might have a long way to feel. Some people have a tendency to go much, much too high. They inflate. They go as high as they can go, regardless of truth—and they encourage others to do the same. They do all they can to support a false notion.

*Director:* Plenty believe their own inflated number is true, that they're much higher than they are. So we argue against their notion that two plus two makes fifty, or whatever.

*Professor:* We can do more. We can show them, positively show them, that things don't add up to fifty.

*Actor:* How?

*Professor:* By bringing on a crisis, one that forces them to see.

20

*Director:* I can see how there might be a crisis for those who believe they're more than they are. But what crisis comes when you're too low?

*Professor:* The crisis of not living up to who you are. And that's the harder case.

*Actor:* Why?

*Professor:* Because it's harder to build up than tear down.

*Director:* Not always. The ones who need to build themselves up might be very receptive to what we have to say. And the ones who need to tear themselves down a bit might be deaf. But I can't help but feel we're going astray.

*Actor:* How so?

*Professor:* He wants to limit us to our discussion of ideas.

*Actor:* But we're talking about ideas. Ideas of self. And we're saying there's a more than right, a less than right, and a just right. And I'd say this applies to every idea, self or not.

*Professor:* Not every idea. Nothingness can't be more, less, or just so. What would it mean to have just the right nothing?

*Actor:* Haven't you ever heard people say 'nothing too much'?

*Professor:* Yes, but it's not the same thing.

*Director:* How would you summarize the idea of nothing?

*Professor:* Nothing is the idea to which no qualities may be ascribed.

*Actor:* Okay. But nothing either exists or it doesn't. If it exists, we ascribe the quality of being.

*Director:* You're making progress as a philosopher, I see.

*Professor:* Yes, he is. But we have to ask—is being the ultimate idea?

*Actor:* Let's say yes.

*Professor:* So every idea has being?

*Actor:* Of course.

*Professor:* The more, the less, the just right—they all exist as ideas?

*Actor:* They all have being.

*Professor:* Which of them has being when two plus two equals four?

*Actor:* The just right.

*Professor:* The more and the less don't exist here?

*Actor:* No, but they exist elsewhere.

*Professor:* Even if all the math in the world is good?

*Actor:* What do you mean?

*Professor:* If ten plus ten always equals twenty, and so on, for all the math in everyone's thoughts and deeds—do more and less exist?

*Actor:* Twenty is more than ten. Ten is less than twenty.

*Professor:* You're slipping away from the point.

*Actor:* I admit I've lost the point.

*Director:* Is this the point, Professor? That more and less only exist, for our purposes, when something isn't right. You've gone too high or too low.

*Professor:* Yes.

*Actor:* So we're using more and less in a special sense.

*Professor:* We are. We're using it in the sense of knowing things for what they are. We're talking about the idea of measurement.

*Actor:* Then why not use too high and too low instead of more and less?

*Director:* I think that's a good idea. And I like thinking about the idea of measurement. But tell us, Professor. What can't be measured?

*Professor:* Nothingness.

*Actor:* But we can measure empty space.

*Professor:* Space is something.

*Actor:* Oh, you're grasping.

*Professor:* Why? Space is a concept. A concept is something.

*Actor:* Nothingness is a concept. Is nothingness something?

*Professor:* Nothingness is the absence of something, of anything.

*Director:* Let's get back to measurement. Are we certain all else but nothingness can be measured?

*Professor:* I can't think of anything that can't. Can you?

*Actor:* What about things that know no bounds?

*Professor:* Can you give an example?

*Actor:* Sure, the character I'm working on now says his hatred for his enemy knows no bounds. Can we measure the hatred?

*Professor:* Essentially, you're asking about the idea of infinity.

*Actor:* I am?

*Professor:* You are. Infinity is the opposite of nothingness. It's an immeasurable something, something so much it knows no limit.

*Actor:* But, like nothingness, it either is or isn't.

*Director:* How can we know it is?

*Professor:* I don't think we can.

*Actor:* So either we believe in infinity or we don't, and we'll never know if our belief is true?

*Director:* Well, we can know if it's false. We come to the end.

*Actor:* Yes, of course. We come to the end. But is that how we know if our idea of nothingness is false? We come to the beginning?

*Director:* Not necessarily the beginning. We just come to something, at whatever stage of being it's in.

### 21

*Professor:* Actor, what's the opposite of being?

*Actor:* You want me to say it's nothingness.

*Professor:* Yes, but there's another opposite. Becoming.

*Actor:* That's an opposite that has to do with time, which is a kind of measurement.

*Professor:* Yes, that's true.

*Actor:* Time means nothing to nothingness.

*Professor:* I agree.

*Actor:* And nothingness can't become anything other than what it is.

*Professor:* Nothingness has no becoming.

*Actor:* But is nothingness eternal?

*Professor:* We can't know.

*Actor:* Somehow I find that encouraging.

*Professor:* So do I.

*Director:* Why do you two find it encouraging?

*Actor:* Because death, possibly the ultimate nothingness, might not be eternal. We can believe one way or the other—but we can't know.

*Professor:* There's comfort in not knowing.

*Director:* When you take comfort in not knowing, do you only take comfort in the things that can't be known?

*Professor:* Of course. Everything I can know I want to know. But we have to be careful here.

*Director:* Why?

*Professor:* Just as I say there's comfort in not knowing, there are those who say there's comfort in knowing.

*Director:* Isn't there?

*Professor:* Of course there is! But think of the incentive.

*Director:* The incentive to know?

*Professor:* The incentive to believe you can know what you can't.

*Director:* And I suppose the opposite holds as well.

*Professor:* Yes, there's incentive to believe you can't know what you can.

*Director:* Then we'd better be clear. How do we know when something can't be known?

*Professor:* The idea of the unknowable? It's the opposite of the idea of the knowable. And that idea, of knowledge, is this—anything that's a thing can be known.

*Actor:* So nothing—no-thing—is all that can't be known? But what about infinity? It's a thing, though a special sort of thing. Can we know it?

*Professor:* Yes.

*Director:* How?

*Professor:* I should clarify. We can know the effect of infinity on us. That's how we know infinity.

*Director:* That's how we know the belief in infinity, you mean.

*Professor:* Yes. And I'll explain. The infinite can't be measured. Well, what if you believe lots of things can't be measured—things that actually can? And what may be worse, what if you mislead people into believing lots of things can't be measured—things that actually can?

*Actor:* You're talking about an abuse of the idea of infinity.

*Professor:* Precisely. We often apply the infinite to non-infinite things.

*Actor:* So if someone says, 'There are infinite reasons not to do this thing,' it may actually be that there's only one reason, and not a very good one at that.

*Director:* This abuse of infinity leads to bad results.

*Professor:* Of course it does.

*Director:* So we shouldn't take it lightly if someone takes non-infinite things and makes them infinite.

*Professor:* Not lightly at all. It leads to a sort of giving up, a sort of helpless hopelessness.

*Actor:* Then that's what we should fight.

22

*Director:* Yes, that's a good fight. And I think that's a nice way to end our talk about what we can call the basic ideas.

*Actor:* Now I want to talk about practical ideas.

*Professor:* What's the idea behind the word 'practical'?

*Actor:* Utility.

*Professor:* The basic ideas aren't useful?

*Actor:* Yes, they are, but they should go without saying. They're the ultimate generalities. To live we need the particular.

*Director:* You mean we need to get political.

*Actor:* Political? I'm not sure that follows.

*Professor:* Director means political in the broadest sense, the sense of the ancients. He wants us to talk about citizens and the state—the sort of state, like a city-state, which encompasses a person's whole life.

*Actor:* But that's not how we think of the state. Our conception is narrower. We distinguish between state and society.

*Professor:* The ancients would say our state and society combined amounts to a city-state like regime. And I think they're right.

*Actor:* Would they say the public and private combine in the same way?

*Professor:* Certainly.

*Actor:* Then thank goodness we're not living in ancient times! From what you're saying they politicized everything.

*Director:* Even every idea.

*Professor:* Don't we do the same?

*Actor:* Hardly. We have apolitical ideas. Just ask those who refuse to vote.

*Professor:* I'm not so sure not voting is apolitical.

*Actor:* What is apolitical, in your opinion?

*Professor:* That which in no way touches on politics.

*Actor:* And that's refusing to vote.

*Professor:* No. Not voting affects the outcome of the vote.

*Actor:* Under the assumption that the outcome would have been different if you voted, sure. But that assumption isn't necessarily true.

*Professor:* Okay. But not voting affects the political climate.

*Actor:* In what way?

*Professor:* Take the simplest way. You tell your friends and family you didn't vote. That might affect the way they think about voting.

*Actor:* It might, yes. But maybe it wouldn't.

*Professor:* Then it will affect the climate at a macro level. The number of non-voters surely affects the way some people think.

*Actor:* And what people think affects the climate.

*Professor:* Of course. That's what the climate is—what people think.

*Actor:* Then everything affects the climate since everything affects what people think!

*Professor:* True.

*Actor:* So all ideas are political, since ideas affect what we think.

*Professor:* Ideas are what we think.

*Director:* Are we really saying all our thoughts are political?

*Actor:* No, apolitical thoughts are apolitical. But they affect the political, in however a round about way.

*Director:* How about the idea of love? That seems as far from the political as we can get.

*Professor:* Love can affect the political.

*Actor:* How?

*Professor:* Suppose the president falls in love. And suppose the beloved has strong political views. Might the president not be swayed?

*Actor:* Sure, I'm certain that sort of thing happens all the time—and not just with those in office.

*Director:* Why doesn't the president sway the other?

*Actor:* I'm sure he or she can. But it all depends.

*Director:* On what?

*Actor:* Which one is more in love than the other.

## 23

*Director:* The one more in love always adopts the beloved's views?

*Actor:* Not always. But there's a tendency that way, a sort of magnetic force.

*Director:* But surely you've heard of couples who belong to different political parties. They can still love each other, can't they?

*Professor:* They can love each other still. But their disagreement is superficial.

*Actor:* How so?

*Professor:* Our political parties agree on more than they differ.

*Actor:* Maybe once that was true. But today? I doubt it.

*Director:* So maybe love across parties can't be?

*Actor:* Love can be if it runs deep.

*Professor:* They're drawn to each other in their cores, and they unite—but they differ on the periphery.

*Director:* The periphery being the political.

*Professor:* Yes.

*Director:* Can love push the political to the periphery when the political occupies a central place?

*Actor:* I think it's possible.

*Director:* Can the political push love to the periphery?

*Actor:* Yes, and it's a terrible thing.

*Director:* Can the political alone do this, or does it take something more?

*Actor:* It takes ambition.

*Director:* Love versus ambition.

*Actor:* Yes.

*Director:* You have ambitions as an actor.

*Actor:* I do.

*Director:* Is ambition central to your heart?

*Actor:* Of course not.

*Director:* You'd sacrifice ambition for love?

*Actor:* I have. But it's not so cut and dry. It's not like love extinguishes the flame of ambition. Good love doesn't, at least. But love can affect ambition.

*Professor:* We need an example.

*Actor:* I turned down a great part that would have required me to be away for a year, because my love couldn't come with me. I chose to stay and find something else that would keep us together.

*Professor:* Did you find something?

*Actor:* I did. And it turned out even better.

*Professor:* Better for your ambition?

*Actor:* Yes.

*Professor:* I'd like to hear of a choice where it turned out worse, as far as ambition goes.

*Actor:* Well, I don't have an example of that from my own life.

*Professor:* I think when someone is truly ambitious, they never choose against it. Sure, they'll go through contortions for love—but love is never enough.

*Actor:* That's an awful thing to say. There are so many ambitious people out there.

*Director:* People want success.

*Actor:* Yes.

*Director:* In whatever thing.

*Actor:* Whatever they set their heart on.

*Director:* Can you be ambitious in love?

*Actor:* You mean, you want your love to succeed?

*Director:* Yes. That's not a political desire, is it?

*Actor:* No, hardly.

*Director:* So you work at your love.

*Actor:* Yes.

*Director:* And if you want your love to succeed more than you want political success?

*Actor:* You're wise.

*Professor:* Yes, but what does it mean to succeed in love?

*Actor:* To have a happy relationship. Happiness is the crown on love.

*Professor:* But if you fail you still have the love?

*Actor:* Well, unhappiness corrodes your relations.

*Professor:* Can the unhappiness be because of thwarted ambition?

*Actor:* Sure.

*Professor:* Political ambition?

*Actor:* Broadly speaking? Yes. And that's how the political can ruin your love.

24

*Director:* Let's get back to the idea of love. What is it?

*Actor:* I'm not sure love can be an idea. In fact, if love becomes an idea—I'm not sure it's still love.

*Director:* Why not?

*Actor:* Love is something you feel, not something you think.

*Professor:* Just as pain is something you feel, not something you think?

*Actor:* Just as pleasure is something you feel, not something you think.

*Director:* Some people experience pain from thinking; and some people experience pleasure in thought.

*Actor:* Yes, but they still feel the pain and pleasure. Love is different. Thinking about love won't make you feel love.

*Director:* Fair enough. So love is something you feel. But what is that feeling? That's the idea of love, the description of that feeling. No?

*Professor:* Yes. That idea is how we can understand what it means for someone to be in love.

*Director:* It's how we can understand not just 'someone', but ourselves to be in love.

*Professor:* Without the idea we would just feel we know not what.

*Actor:* We're better off without the idea.

*Professor:* Why?

*Actor:* The idea can distract us from the reality.

*Professor:* What if we allow the reality to become the idea?

*Actor:* Something is always lost in translation.

*Director:* Then what is love?

*Actor:* Attraction.

*Director:* It's a sort of magnetic force?

*Actor:* Yes, exactly. Sometimes it's weak; sometimes it's strong.

*Professor:* So love relies on the idea of more or less. We measure our love.

*Actor:* We can measure. But we're measuring a feeling, not an idea of the mind. Feelings are of the heart.

*Director:* The physical heart?

*Actor:* You want me to say we feel love in the mind. And we do, in part. But it's not thought, not even a little. It's a feeling through and through.

*Director:* What's the problem with the thinking mind?

*Actor:* It drowns feelings in thought—which, incidentally, makes the thoughts untrue.

*Professor:* I think feeling more often drowns thought.

*Director:* However that may be, is it accurate to say that we can keep the mind pure by being true to our feelings?

*Actor:* Yes, that's exactly true.

*Director:* And that's because feelings are truth?

*Actor:* Yes. Feelings are fundamental facts.

*Director:* And thought is reasoning on facts.

*Actor:* Of course. So we should base our thoughts on feelings.

*Director:* But sometimes we act on feelings without thought?

*Actor:* True. If we're attracted to someone, we should let our thoughts go, and allow ourselves to draw near.

*Director:* And if we're attracted to someone new ten times a day, we should let go and draw near each time?

*Actor:* You think I'll object. But I won't.

*Director:* That's fine. But let's say you approach one of these ten and speak with them, and they're terribly shallow. Might that ruin the attraction?

*Actor:* Certainly.

*Director:* Would you say that's a mental repulsion?

*Actor:* Sure.

*Director:* But it's also a bodily repulsion, because mind is part of body.

*Actor:* We can say that if you like.

*Director:* And what about ideas?

*Actor:* What about them?

*Director:* Do the shallow have many ideas?

*Actor:* I think they can. But they haven't thought them through.

*Director:* The deep have thought them through?

*Actor:* The deep are always thinking.

*Director:* You're attracted to the deep?

*Actor:* I am.

*Director:* But you can only know if someone is deep by talking to them.

*Actor:* True.

*Director:* So it's possible to have false attractions.

*Actor:* What do you mean?

25

*Director*: I mean, you think you're attracted but you're not. You see someone and feel attraction. But when you speak with that person the attraction vanishes. False attraction.

*Actor*: But I really felt the attraction.

*Professor*: It's probably because of an idea.

*Actor*: What idea?

*Professor*: You see someone and imagine they think certain thoughts. You have the idea that they think certain thoughts, deep thoughts.

*Actor*: How did I get this idea?

*Professor*: I don't know. Maybe you want the beauty of the mind to match the beauty of the body.

*Actor*: So when the person doesn't live up to my idea, there's no attraction?

*Professor*: Yes.

*Director*: But not everyone holds to this higher standard. They don't care about depth of mind. To them, body is all.

*Actor*: Why do you think one person cares about an idea and others don't?

*Professor*: Because.

*Actor*: That's the answer?

*Professor*: 'Why' is only answered by 'because'—and 'because' is always an idea.

*Director*: So what does this mean for love? Should we love without because?

*Actor*: I like that. Love just is, yes. No because. After all, who has the right to ask love why?

*Director*: I wonder if we can take this further. Should we do away with all because?

*Professor*: That's as much as to do away with all ideas.

*Director*: Because all ideas are a because?

*Professor*: Yes. Look at justice, for instance. When we punish someone we have to say why. Justice is the because.

*Actor*: But there's no need for a reason why. You killed illegally, for instance, so we punish you. We don't need some other idea.

*Professor*: But we need the idea of illegality. That idea provides the because.

*Director*: I think Professor has a point. We do need ideas. 'Why' is one of the first things a human child asks. It wants to know. It wants ideas.

*Professor:* True, and it's often a shame.

*Actor:* A shame?

*Professor:* Children are defenseless to bad ideas. Most are, at least. And once the seeds are sown, it takes a lifetime to root them out.

### 26

*Director:* What if things are tangled up?

*Actor:* Good ideas with bad?

*Director:* Yes. How can we untangle them?

*Professor:* We can do without an idea, the idea that ties them all up.

*Actor:* What idea?

*Professor:* Justice.

*Actor:* What? You can't be serious.

*Professor:* Don't you think justice is the key idea? What did we say? Justice is getting what you deserve? What's more important than that?

*Actor:* I still don't think you're serious. But I'll play along. What would we do? Simply feel what we and others deserve? No idea of justice involved? It would be a catastrophe.

*Director:* Why?

*Actor:* Because everyone feels that they deserve something great!

*Director:* And that others deserve less than they have?

*Actor:* Of course!

*Director:* There would be conflict over this?

*Actor:* Certainly!

*Director:* So what do we need?

*Actor:* Laws.

*Director:* We replace justice with the legal?

*Actor:* Yes, but we need to make the laws just.

*Director:* So we need an idea of justice to help us frame laws.

*Actor:* True.

*Director:* Is justice pure idea?

*Actor:* No, sometimes justice is more than pure idea. Sometimes justice is done.

*Director:* Justice is a good verdict, for instance?

*Actor:* A good verdict is just.

*Director:* The verdict is the thing. Justice is the idea.

*Actor:* But it's not some perfectly abstract idea.

*Director:* The verdict is the noun. Just or unjust is the adjective.

*Actor:* Right.

*Director:* Are all ideas adjectives? And we're not talking about this in a strictly grammatical way.

*Actor:* No, I know what you mean. We're saying something like, are all ideas means to measure, means to determine quality?

*Director:* Are they?

*Actor:* I don't know.

*Professor:* I do. And the answer is, yes. Even nothingness gets at this in its own way. Nothingness means no measure, no quality.

*Actor:* So if there were no idea of measure-and-quality, nothingness wouldn't exist?

*Professor:* Ah, you put the hard question. Let's just say they go together.

*Actor:* Nothingness depends on at least one other idea.

*Professor:* Well, if that idea didn't exist it might be fair to say nothingness is all.

*Actor:* But then we wouldn't be here to say it.

*Director:* So it's a good thing measure-and-quality exists. But let's get back to our question. Are all ideas adjectives?

*Professor:* In the classical sense, ideas are the timeless blueprints for time-bound things. The time-bound things succeed or fail according to how well they match the blueprints. I'm not sure I'd call that adjectival.

*Director:* But in the modern sense?

*Actor:* There are no timeless blueprints. We make the blueprints ourselves.

*Director:* What difference does that make?

*Actor:* None, really. The only concern in either case is how good a match we make.

*Director:* So there's an idea of matching.

*Actor:* Or accuracy, or something along those lines, yes.

*Professor:* Could it be an idea of precision?

*Actor:* Sure, precision. I think that's right.

*Director:* Could things have played out like this? Humans got better and better at matching timeless blueprints, until they realized the limitations of those blueprints—so they decided to make their own.

*Actor:* Yes, but what are we talking about? The blueprint of a house? Or the blueprint of... justice?

### 27

*Director:* Does it matter?

*Actor:* Houses admit of precision in the making. Justice doesn't.

*Director:* Why not? Justice is done or it isn't. One or zero. Binary. No?

*Actor:* We can never say with precision what someone deserves. We can only approximate justice.

*Professor:* Why?

*Actor:* Because precision here requires absolute knowledge.

*Professor:* Plenty of people seem to think they have absolute knowledge regarding justice.

*Actor:* And that's the problem. They think they know what justice is in each particular case.

*Director:* But the laws are clear. Or are you talking about something more?

*Actor:* You know I am.

*Director:* You're talking about something like karma?

*Actor:* Yes, knowledge of the sum of all a person's experiences and actions. That's what justice requires. And that's why justice is imprecise—because we can never know all this.

*Professor:* If we can never know, why set that as the standard?

*Actor:* Because ideas can serve as ideals—something to strive toward.

*Professor:* Your ideal here, perfect knowledge, is often attributed to God.

*Actor:* I don't believe in God.

*Professor:* But you apparently believe in godlike omniscience.

*Actor:* Like I said, it's an ideal—a human ideal. And I believe humans knew of this ideal before they knew of God. In fact, God may have come of this ideal.

*Director:* So justice isn't binary—done or not. There are degrees, or shades, of justice as far as this goes.

*Actor:* Yes.

*Director:* When there's no justice, what's the color of the shade?

*Actor:* Black.

*Director:* Really? And when there's complete justice?

*Actor:* White.

*Director:* And everything between is some sort of gray?

*Actor:* Yes.

*Professor:* Then ideas can be described in two ways. They're either a matter of more or less, or they're a matter of yes or no.

*Director:* Can we divide ideas according to these descriptions, or is each idea a matter of both? Do you know what I'm asking?

*Actor:* I know. Take the idea of being alive. We're either living or dead, yes or no. But some of the living are less than fully alive, if you know what I mean. They're partly dead inside.

*Professor:* Yes, so I'd say the idea of life is a matter of more or less, as well as yes or no.

*Director:* Then what's a simple yes or no?

*Professor:* I think all political things, justice aside, are yes or no.

*Actor:* To set justice aside is to remove the core.

*Professor:* Yes, but consider—you're either a citizen or not, a permanent resident or not, a visa holder or not.

*Actor:* That's true.

*Professor:* And you're either old enough to vote, serve in the military, or hold office—or not.

*Actor:* You have a license to hunt or fish, or not.

*Professor:* Yes, and we can go on.

*Actor:* You win the election, or not. The law passes, or not. The law is upheld, or not. We can go on. So I agree, most political things are yes or no.

*Professor:* Can you think of anything political, besides justice, that isn't a yes or no?

*Actor:* I... can't. Can you, Director?

*Director:* I'm still amazed that we may have discovered a truth about the political. No, I can't think of anything right now. Unless...

*Actor:* Unless what?

*Director:* ...we come back to war. Are we always truly either at war or not? Or are there stages in-between?

*Actor:* We can certainly take hostile actions during peace. And we can fight undeclared wars. And then there are trade wars and other such things. Are they so very clear cut?

*Director:* Yes, I think there can be gray here. Professor?

*Professor:* It seems war and justice are the exceptions.

*Actor:* And even when we're at war, there's limited war and total war.

*Director:* A good point. Is there any other political thing that allows for gray?

*Actor:* I think those are the two. Oh, and Director?

*Director:* Yes?

*Actor:* I think we should include civil war here.

*Director:* Of course.

*Actor:* And class warfare.

*Director:* A type of civil war, yes. Anything else?

*Actor:* That's it.

## 28

*Director:* What's the most important apolitical idea, and is it yes or no?

*Professor:* There's more than one—those of mathematics.

*Actor:* The political makes use of mathematical ideas.

*Professor:* Yes, if only in counting citizens, money, or votes. But mathematics doesn't make use of the political.

*Director:* Are we sure about that? What if politics surreptitiously colors our mathematical ideas?

*Professor:* I'd need to see the proof.

*Director:* Okay. But let's get back to the question. Are mathematical ideas matters of yes or no, or are they matters of more or less?

*Professor:* It depends on the idea.

*Actor:* Give us an example of an idea that's more or less.

*Professor:* The idea of the equal.

*Actor:* How so?

*Professor:* Can one thing ever truly equal another? Truly?

*Actor:* No, I know what you mean. No two actual things are ever perfectly alike. Equality, outside the abstractions of math, is an ideal we approximate.

*Professor:* So equality is like justice, a matter of degree.

*Director:* But what happens when we bring the idea of the equal into politics?

*Professor:* It turns into a matter of yes or no. Yes, we're equal before the law; no, we're not.

*Actor:* Equality is an apolitical idea made political. But politics ruins it.

*Director:* How?

*Actor:* You know the old saying. We're all equal here—but some are more equal than others.

*Director:* We want equality to be yes-or-no.

*Actor:* We want politics to be like math. Math upholds the idea. Politics doesn't.

*Professor:* But haven't you ever heard of anti-ideal mathematics?

*Actor:* No, I haven't.

*Professor:* This sort of mathematics tries to take into account what happens outside the realm of the ideal.

*Actor:* And it does this by being less than ideal?

*Professor:* Yes. It's answers are only partly true.

*Director:* Can we apply the anti-ideal to non-mathematical ideals, as well?

*Professor:* Of course we can. To equality, for instance.

*Director:* So we can approach equality in the anti-ideal mode in order to solve real world problems the best we can.

*Professor:* Right. We seek to maximize the equality we have. We never reach perfection, but we do pretty well.

*Director:* How else can the anti-ideal serve politics?

*Professor:* Generally speaking? It comes up with anti-ideal theories of ideals.

*Director:* So it might create an anti-ideal theory of justice?

*Professor:* Yes, of course. And it's been done.

*Actor:* Is the theory any good?

*Professor:* It's been done more than once. Each time it gives something to everyone and satisfies none.

*Actor:* People crave the ideal.

*Director:* Not all do.

*Actor:* What do they crave?

*Director:* Often times? They crave a good meal.

*Actor:* Oh, come on.

*Director:* Alright. Then tell me. Which do you think they crave more—justice or love?

*Actor:* Love.

*Director:* He didn't even hesitate, Professor.

*Professor:* No, he didn't. But he might if we speak of the anti-ideal of love.

## 29

*Actor:* Why would anyone want an anti-ideal of love?

*Professor:* They want the best they can get.

*Actor:* I'd never settle for that.

*Director:* You want the worst you can get?

*Actor:* No, of course not.

*Professor:* Humor us, Actor. Tell us how you'd live if you settled.

*Actor:* That's a big 'if'. But I'd take things up to the ideal as often as I could. That would keep me going.

*Director:* Romantic get-aways and so on?

*Actor:* Yes, but mostly and-so-on.

*Director:* And what about when it comes to justice? The same?

*Actor:* Sure, we can take ourselves to the ideal now and then. That would keep people in the game.

*Director:* In the game?

*Actor:* They don't stop playing along.

*Professor:* I'm not sure I like the way that sounds.

*Actor:* You're the one who gave us the idea of the imperfect ideal.

*Director:* Yes. But what are we saying? There are important moments in love and justice that make it all worthwhile?

*Actor:* Right. The love isn't perfect. But it's sometimes close. And there are perfect moments along the way.

*Professor:* That's how it is with everything. The perfect is fleeting. We live with the imperfect. And some 'imperfects' are better than others.

*Director:* Which would you rather have? An imperfect that's fifty percent of the way toward perfect, with ten perfect moments a year; or an imperfect that's seventy-five percent of the way toward perfect with five perfect moments a year?

*Professor:* I'd rather have neither. And here's why. Consider my class. Students who are seventy-five percent of the way toward perfect knowledge are more likely to have more perfect moments than students who are only fifty percent of the way there. More is more.

*Actor:* But how can you know that? What if the effort to take things to seventy-five percent exhausts the students? They have nothing left for those perfect moments.

*Director:* Actor has a point. Besides, I have a suspicion.

*Professor:* What suspicion?

*Director:* That the idea of perfect knowledge, or perfect whatever—reaching one hundred percent—is nothing but a carrot on a stick, used to manipulate, to urge people ever on.

*Professor:* What's wrong with that?

*Actor:* People should know the truth about one hundred percent. And they should have sub-ideas.

*Director:* Sub-ideas?

*Actor:* Ideas below ideas on the general level.

*Professor:* General like justice or love.

*Actor:* Yes. We create these sub-ideas ourselves. They motivate us toward the general ideas, but on our own terms—and not as a carrot.

*Director:* How do they motivate us?

*Actor:* They suit our own circumstances and needs.

*Professor:* Custom made ideas.

*Actor:* That's right.

*Professor:* But think of it this way. When we buy a suit, an actual suit—something much less important than an idea—we often have a professional tailor cut the suit to fit. Likewise, why not have a professional suit us with ideas?

*Director:* Don't tell us. That's what a teacher does.

*Professor:* Yes. At the least, a teacher can help take the measurements.

*Actor:* I don't know. I'd rather measure and suit myself.

*Professor:* Many who have that opinion often end up doing something sad.

*Actor:* What?

*Professor:* They buy their suits ready to wear, off the rack.

*Director:* Some people have the right size for the rack. Others need custom fitting.

*Actor:* I would never take my ideas off the rack.

*Professor:* Doesn't it depend on the idea? Political ideas are often off the rack. One size fits all, no?

*Actor:* No, I don't agree. One size never fits all.

*Professor:* So what would you have? Will the legislature tailor its ideas for you?

*Actor:* You know that won't happen.

*Director:* Oh, I don't know. Doesn't the legislature tailor ideas today?

*Actor:* How so?

*Director:* Consider the tax code. Those making this much money pay this; those making that much money pay that; and there are many exceptions tailored to certain types of people.

*Actor:* You have a point.

*Professor:* Yes, and that opens the door to other tailorings here and there. But for the most part, laws in an equality-minded society apply equally to all, which makes the laws one-size-fits-all.

*Director:* Actor, you said one-size-fits-all really doesn't fit us all. Are you saying while your fellow citizens are prohibited from stealing, for instance, you should be free to take what you like?

*Actor:* Of course not. I'm thinking more of things like public education. They're one-size-fits-all, but shouldn't be.

*Professor:* But there are private schools; there's home schooling. There are ways around.

*Actor:* Yes, but there are many laws you can't get around without breaking them.

*Professor:* Name one you would break.

*Actor:* Let me give you some context first. On Sundays when I was growing up, we had dinner at my grandparents' home. When I turned thirteen they started serving me a small glass of wine with my meal. This had always been their way, going back many generations. I learned that wine should enliven and spur conversation. I didn't learn to abuse.

*Director:* So the drinking age law of twenty-one, that didn't fit.

*Actor:* It did not.

*Director:* It prohibited your tradition.

*Actor:* Senselessly, I might add.

*Director:* So you chose to break the law. Why weren't you caught?

*Actor:* What were the police going to do? Break down my grandparents' door and storm the table?

*Director:* Do you think even if they knew what was going on, some might turn a blind eye?

*Actor:* Yes, because it was innocent. It was training me to be an adult.

*Director:* Your family acted responsibly in giving you only so much?

*Actor:* Yes. And they made sure I knew not to have any anywhere else.

*Professor:* Not every family approaches things this way.

*Actor:* And that's why we have the law.

## 30

*Director:* Is that the idea of law? It should pick up where families leave off?

*Actor:* That's one idea of law.

*Director:* What's another?

*Actor:* It should be a rational set of rules that support human excellence.

*Director:* What, like patent and copyright laws? They encourage invention and creativity?

*Actor:* Sure.

*Director:* Could one law support one idea of law, and another law support another?

*Actor:* Of course.

*Director:* Could the ideas stand in conflict?

*Actor:* No doubt they could.

*Director:* Then there'd be tension in the law?

*Actor:* Yes.

*Director:* What happens when there's tension in the law?

*Actor:* People feel tension.

*Director:* Necessarily?

*Actor:* Tell me why they wouldn't.

*Director:* Well, they might feel tension, but it might be less tension.

*Actor:* Why?

*Director:* Do you agree there are more ideas of law than the two we mentioned?

*Actor:* I do.

*Director:* One of them might be the tyrannical idea.

*Actor:* True.

*Director:* If that idea of law were dominant, and we came along with another idea, what would happen?

*Actor:* We'd be in trouble.

*Director:* Why?

*Actor:* Because the tyrannical idea is that the tyrant is above the law. Every other idea of law opposes this view. That's why we'd be in trouble.

*Director:* But if we managed to pass our law?

*Actor:* We might rein the tyrant, or tyrants, in.

*Director:* If we don't completely rein them in, there would be tension, no?

*Actor:* Of course there would. Our idea against theirs.

*Director:* What would come of this tension? Anything good?

*Actor:* It would be better than having the tyrannical idea alone. So, yes, I'd say something good comes of this tension.

*Director:* Does this good only happen when it comes to laws?

*Actor:* No, it can happen with many sorts of tyrannical ideas. We resist the tyranny through new ideas.

*Professor:* Or old ideas brought back to life.

*Actor:* Yes, even through old ideas. And that's good because then it doesn't matter if we're conservative or progressive—we can find our idea and resist.

*Director:* It might even be good to hit tyranny from both sides.

*Actor:* It would be good. And I think that's the only time conservatives and progressives unite.

*Professor:* In a war of ideas.

*Actor:* In a war of the people who believe the ideas.

*Professor:* Still, it's war by means of ideas.

*Actor:* People can use other means to support their ideas.

*Professor:* Like violence?

*Actor:* Like violence.

*Professor:* If an idea is good, does it need violent support?

*Actor:* Sometimes in self-defense, yes.

*Director:* When someone attacks an idea through violent means, do they do it in the name of another idea?

*Actor:* Of course.

*Director:* But can they really hope to force others to believe?

*Actor:* They can force others to act like they believe. But no, you can't force belief.

*Director:* Why would you want someone to act like they believe?

*Actor:* The more that act like they believe, the more likely it is that some will come to believe.

*Director:* Why?

*Actor:* Because ideas are contagious through acts.

*Director:* Act as though you believe often enough and you may well come to believe?

*Actor:* Yes, but what's more likely is that those close to you might come to believe.

*Director:* So philosophy must concern itself with acts.

*Professor:* That's how philosophers open themselves to attack.

*Director:* They open themselves in order to attack?

*Professor:* What? No! They make themselves vulnerable.

*Director:* By concerning themselves with acts instead of ideas.

*Professor:* Oh, they're still concerned with ideas. But meddling in acts does them in.

*Director:* But you're not being fair.

*Professor:* What do you mean?

*Director:* Would you say that in your class there are no acts, only ideas?

*Professor:* Well, now you've got me.

*Actor:* How so?

*Professor:* Director knows that engaging with ideas is an act.

*Actor:* Yes, but it's not the same sort of thing as performing actual acts.

*Professor:* Isn't it? What do you think happens when I meet with a class in which everyone believes in a bad idea?

*Actor:* You try to correct them?

*Professor:* Yes. Wouldn't you say that's an act? A very important act?

*Actor:* Alright, it's an act. But what's the nature of this act? What do you do?

*Professor:* I ask them questions, questions that loosen them up.

*Actor:* And when they're loose?

*Professor:* They don't take the bad idea as seriously.

*Actor:* And then you encourage them to change their view?

*Professor:* Yes.

*Actor:* That might work in a free society. But you couldn't do that in a tyranny, you know.

*Professor:* In a tyranny you spread the questions out. You don't hit the students all at once.

*Actor:* So what you're doing is less noticeable?

*Professor:* And safer, too.

### 31

*Director:* What are we looking for when we question?

*Actor:* Whether an idea can stand up to questions.

*Director:* We want our ideas to admit no doubt?

*Actor:* No, an idea can be doubted and still stand tall.

*Director:* And when it stands tall, we're more likely to act on it?

*Actor:* Yes.

*Director:* So it's not a problem if you have doubts, for instance, about a character you play.

*Actor:* That's no problem at all. The character himself may have self-doubt.

*Director:* And if the character has no doubt?

*Actor:* It's usually not worth acting the part—because lack of doubt isn't very interesting.

*Director:* Doubt makes things interesting?

*Actor:* Of course.

*Director:* And not just on stage? I mean, doubt in real life is interesting?

*Professor:* It certainly is. I have the most interesting exchanges with my students when they admit to their doubts.

*Director:* But where do we go from doubt? Do we try to arrive at certainty?

*Professor:* Yes. But if we're honest with ourselves, we know there's precious little of that. For the most part we live in a world where some doubts are simply less than others.

*Actor:* But there is certainty.

*Professor:* True, but most of the certain have doubts they won't admit.

*Director:* Won't admit to others or themselves?

*Professor:* Both.

*Director:* What happens if you press them on the doubts you think they have?

*Professor:* They often get upset.

*Director:* If they get upset, do you know you've found an un-admitted doubt?

*Professor:* Chances are good.

*Director:* So what do you do then?

*Professor:* I back off, and try again when they've cooled down.

*Director:* And when you try again, what do you do?

*Professor:* I find ways to gently nourish the doubt.

*Actor:* What does it mean to nourish a doubt?

*Professor:* To build awareness.

*Director:* Awareness is good. That's an idea I'm fairly certain about.

*Actor:* But you're not completely certain?

*Director:* No, I'm not. Awareness taken to an extreme might be less than good. And, now that I'm at it, partial awareness might be worse than being unaware.

*Actor:* You don't really believe that.

*Director:* No, I don't. It's just a doubt I sometimes have.

*Professor:* You admit the doubt. That's healthy. So there's no need to nourish it here.

*Actor:* Is that what your philosophy is? Nurture of doubt?

*Professor:* In large part, yes. But doubts can lead us to certainty.

*Actor:* Is that the goal of philosophy? Certainty?

*Professor:* We can say it's philosophy's ideal—something hard to obtain, but something we strive toward with all our might.

*Actor:* So what is this? Skepticism? The idea that knowledge to a certainty is impossible?

*Professor:* No, it's possible. It's simply rare.

*Actor:* But you try to tear everything down, to render doubt wherever you go.

*Professor:* True, but some things can't be torn down; some things admit no doubt. And that, Actor, is what I want everyone to see.

### 32

*Actor:* Then what? We flock to the certainty of the can't-be-torn-down?

*Professor:* Assuming the can't-be-torn-down isn't a bad idea.

*Actor:* And if it is?

*Professor:* We look for good ideas that are certain enough to stand up to the bad.

*Actor:* Certain enough?

*Professor:* When you're at war you learn to make do with what you have.

*Actor:* Some war you fight—sparring with helpless students.

*Professor:* They're far from helpless. And we do more than spar. Something real is at stake.

*Actor:* Their ideas.

*Professor:* Yes—and mine, too.

*Actor:* What do their parents think of you?

*Professor:* Some thank me.

*Actor:* For what?

*Professor:* Helping to temper a hot headed youth, for instance.

*Actor:* They were hot headed because they were certain?

*Professor:* Or because they had certain doubts.

*Actor:* You show them it's alright to doubt?

*Professor:* I validate them, as they say.

*Actor:* What about other parents?

*Professor:* Some insist their children drop my class.

*Actor:* And they drop your class?

*Professor:* Some of them, yes.

*Actor:* Don't you try to dissuade them?

*Professor:* On occasion.

*Actor:* Why only on occasion?

*Professor:* If they're willing to drop my class in obedience to their parents, how likely are they to listen to me?

*Actor:* I think you should always try. What harm can come of it?

*Director:* Yes, but there's another point to make.

*Actor:* What point?

*Director:* That the discussions will be better without them.

*Actor:* That's not true. Professor, what can you say to them to win them over?

*Professor:* I can ask them one question. Who knows better what happens in class—your parents or you?

*Actor:* That's enough for some of them to stay?

*Professor:* That's enough.

*Actor:* And the rest? What's the real reason they go?

*Professor:* Aside from obedience? Maybe they don't like doubt.

*Actor:* But really—who likes doubt?

*Professor:* Maybe they can't tolerate doubt.

*Director:* They'd be hard to work with, then.

*Professor:* Yes. So off they go to other professors who love to deal in certainties. They're much more comfortable there.

*Actor:* Is that what it's all about? Comfort?

*Professor:* For them? Maybe it is.

### 33

*Director:* I'm uncomfortable when too many untested certainties are thrown about.

*Professor:* You'd enjoy my class.

*Actor:* Too bad you're too old, Director.

*Director:* What's this? Too old to seek?

*Actor:* Seek? What are you seeking?

*Director:* True certainty.

*Actor:* The real seeking for that happens when you're young.

*Director:* Young in years or young in spirit?

*Professor:* Spirit, of course. And you have the spirit. I'd allow you to sit in on my class.

*Actor:* And if his doubts swallow everyone up?

*Director:* You make me sound like a whale.

*Professor:* If we're swallowed by this whale, we'll strive for certainty all the more—and Director will, too.

*Director:* Who wouldn't strive their best to get out of the belly of the beast?

*Actor:* And that's what we want. Our very best effort toward sound ideas.

*Director:* Sound? Not certain?

*Actor:* Sound means there's more certainty than doubt. Sound ideas are ideas you can live by.

*Director:* I think I like the idea of sound ideas. I think I'll live by the idea of sound ideas!

*Actor:* Is philosophy a sound idea?

*Professor:* Philosophy is the means to determine which ideas are sound.

*Actor:* That sounds sound to me.

*Director:* And to me. But I'll tell you a problem. In all my years as a philosopher, I've yet to find a sound idea that remains sound for long.

*Actor:* Ridiculous!

*Director:* But it's true! I've had to shift from idea to idea like a nomad wandering here and there. Philosophy is the only thing that keeps me going.

*Actor:* But it's impossible to live without ideas.

*Director:* Oh, don't get me wrong. I live with ideas. But I don't believe in them beyond the time they're sound.

*Actor:* But what about the ideas of math? Haven't you lived with the idea of multiplication for long? Surely that's a sound idea.

*Director:* Ah, my ideas about soundness don't seem so sound!

*Professor:* He's just teasing, Actor. When he says he lives with ideas, he means he uses ideas, just as he uses math.

*Actor:* Director, what's another idea you use, aside from those of math?

*Director:* I'm not sure how to put it.

*Actor:* Try.

*Director:* When I see one of your movies, I see you in your role. But I don't believe you've actually become the person I see on the screen. I know you're acting. So I guess I make use of the idea of performance.

*Actor:* But why don't you believe in that idea? I am, after all, performing.

*Director:* Yes, you are. But I think you're also becoming something of the person you represent. And I think you take some of this away with you when you're done. So you're not absolutely performing. You're also becoming, being what you act.

*Actor:* Well, it's true our roles can change us. There is no absolute wall between self and part. If there were, we wouldn't be convincing. But what other ideas do you use?

*Director:* What ideas don't I use?

*Actor:* Okay, but when do you stop using an idea? When do you, the nomad, have to move on?

*Director:* I stop using an idea when the preponderance of the evidence is against it.

*Actor:* Such as?

*Director:* It might seem a good idea to invest my money in a certain stock. But then the evidence mounts that the company isn't doing well. My good idea now seems bad, and I'll stop using it. What, you don't like my example?

*Professor:* I think it didn't seem philosophical enough for Actor.

*Director:* Then substitute the idea of 'friend' for 'company'. And here's the example. I believe we have friendship. But the evidence shows we don't. I'll abandon my belief and move on to better friends.

*Actor:* Yes, but you're not really abandoning the idea of friendship. You're abandoning false friends.

*Director:* What if I tell you I abandon one idea of friendship for another?

*Actor:* That's the more interesting case.

*Director:* Yes, and the new idea will help me find new friends.

*Actor:* Until you abandon that idea.

*Director:* Who says I will? As long as it's sound, I stay with it—doggedly.

*Actor:* Look at you smirk. Why are you joking?

*Director:* Because I want you to think nothing is forever with me.

*Actor:* When in fact everything is forever with you?

*Director:* Not everything, but many things.

*Actor:* Including the multiplication tables?

*Director:* Including them, unless they're somehow proved wrong.

*Actor:* And that's how it is with you? Sound until wrong?

*Director:* Well, certain things have to be proved right before I consider them sound.

*Actor:* Like what?

*Director:* Principles and commitments. If they're sound, I'm with them always.

*Actor:* But people stick with these things even when they're unsound. In fact, they'd say it's when they're unsound that the real test begins.

*Director:* Then I would fail. Would you really stick with a principle you know is bad?

*Actor:* I wouldn't, no.

*Director:* If you were committed to a film, and midway through it becomes clear that it will be a total failure—would you stay on?

*Actor:* My contract would almost certainly lock me in.

*Director:* You'd be punished if you left?

*Actor:* And not just by the contract, yes.

*Director:* Do you want to be associated with a bad film?

*Actor:* Of course not.

*Director:* But considerations of money, and future work, and so on—they would keep you on?

*Actor:* Well, that doesn't sound so good. But really, Director. How can we know, absolutely know, a film will be a flop?

*Director:* I might not know. But I imagine people with experience in these things can tell.

*Actor:* But that's the thing! They can't. No one knows for certain what will be a hit or a miss—or worse.

*Director:* I believe you about hits and misses. But as for 'worse'? I think people can tell. I think you can tell, Actor.

*Actor:* Well, if something is a total disaster, yes—I can tell.

*Director:* Would you keep your commitment to a disaster?

*Actor:* No.

*Director:* Alright. Then don't be so quick to judge me for only doing the same. And it's harder for me.

*Actor:* Harder? You're not under contract.

*Director:* I'm under something more serious.

*Actor:* What?

*Director:* Expectations.

*Actor:* People's expectations of you?

*Director:* Yes! What's more fearsome than that? And I'll tell you what makes it harder.

*Actor:* Please do.

*Director:* Insider trading.

*Actor:* What are you talking about?

*Director:* You remember my example about selling my stock? Well, I often have insider news.

*Actor:* Literally? Securities fraud?

*Director:* No, not that. When it comes to other things, when I go to 'sell', people can't understand why.

### 34

*Actor:* Give them your reasons.

*Director:* I do, but they don't believe me.

*Professor:* Can you give us an example?

*Director:* Let's say I have friend who's an engineer. One day he tells me a certain bridge isn't sound, but for political reasons it stays open. I tell everyone I know not to take the bridge. They ask me why. I tell them it's not sound. They laugh. 'What does Director know?' They take the bridge and one day it falls down.

*Actor:* Your friend had a duty to come forward at large with what he knew.

*Director:* Yes, but he didn't.

*Actor:* Well, I suppose you did what you could, short of going to the authorities. Why didn't you, anyway?

*Professor:* It's just a hypothetical, Actor. But let's be clear about what we're saying. The bridge is an idea?

*Director:* Ideas can be bridges, yes.

*Actor:* Bridges between other ideas?

*Director:* Yes.

*Actor:* Give us an example.

*Director:* The idea of two is a bridge between the ideas of one and three.

*Actor:* Oh, of course. But give us a real example.

*Director:* The idea of film director is a bridge between writer and actor.

*Actor:* I see you really do want to keep to easy examples. That's fine. And it's true. Directors bridge between writers and actors. But come on, we need a better example.

*Director:* I know what you want. You want to hear about justice and love.

*Actor:* Yes!

*Director:* Can love be a bridge to justice?

*Actor:* I suppose love can help someone toward justice. But in general terms? It doesn't sound right.

*Director:* Can justice be a bridge to love?

*Actor:* Again, there might be cases where a just act can lead to love. But in general terms? This doesn't sound right, either.

*Director:* What's the bridge to justice?

*Actor:* A strong sense of fairness.

*Director:* And what's the bridge to love?

*Actor:* Attraction.

*Director:* And what's on the other side, the side that travels over attraction to love?

*Actor:* Worthiness.

*Director:* Ah. The idea of worth.

*Actor:* No, not worth. Worthiness.

*Director:* What's the difference?

*Actor:* You can be worth billions but not be worthy.

*Director:* What might make you worthy?

*Actor:* Having an honest soul.

*Director:* Oh, I see. Worthiness is a quality, not a quantity.

*Actor:* Right. And the worthy cross the bridge of attraction toward love.

### 35

*Director:* I would have thought love would cross the bridge of attraction toward worth.

*Actor:* What difference does it make?

*Professor:* Yes, Director. What difference? Are you trying to complicate things? I know you know that with ideas it's best to keep it simple. After all, the best ideas are simplest of all.

*Director:* The simple is hard.

*Actor:* Is that an excuse?

*Director:* For some it is. Is it for you?

*Actor:* No! I try to master the simple whenever I can.

*Director:* What does it mean to master an idea?

*Actor:* To understand it for what it is from every angle and in every context.

*Director:* Do we try to understand it when combined with other ideas?

*Actor:* I think that's dangerous.

*Professor:* So we need to be monomaniacs? People with one track minds?

*Actor:* Of course not.

*Professor:* But when it's time to think about love it's not time to think about justice?

*Actor:* And the other way round, true.

*Professor:* Director?

*Director:* I'm convinced. And what we're saying even holds in math. When you think about one you shouldn't think about two.

*Professor:* We cannot mix ideas. It makes a mess and gets us into trouble.

*Director:* Just to be sure—what kind of trouble?

*Professor:* Madness.

*Actor:* Madness?

*Professor:* Madmen mix ideas. They try to show everything at once.

*Actor:* Are they mad because they want to show everything at once, or do they want to show everything at once because they're mad?

*Professor:* Does it matter?

*Actor:* We can cure the former, but I don't know what we can do with the latter.

*Director:* How do we cure the former?

*Actor:* We teach them to slow things down, to take their ideas one at a time.

*Director:* Professor, do you often have such madmen in your class?

*Professor:* I do from time to time. And slowing down works.

*Director:* But not all of them slow down?

*Professor:* No, not all of them. Some of them are bursting at the seams to get their ideas out. All I can do is try to focus them on one idea.

*Director:* You have to guess which idea is innermost in their heart?

*Professor:* Exactly. And if I'm right, they concentrate on that and grow better. I usually have them write a thesis on the idea. That takes off some of the pressure. They take the whole year to write it. Plenty of time and no rush, with feedback from me along the way.

*Actor:* What idea is innermost in my heart?

*Professor:* I'm not sure. It could be love. It could be justice. Maybe it's acting or fame. Director, what do you think?

*Director:* I think it's longing for approval.

*Actor:* Hardly. And what's your innermost idea?

*Director:* What do you think it is?

*Professor:* Oh, we all know it's philosophy.

*Actor:* And you, Professor? I don't think it's philosophy for you.

*Professor:* What would it be?

*Actor:* Learning.

*Professor:* What's the difference between learning and philosophy?

*Actor:* There's a large degree of overlap. But, essentially, learning is positive while philosophy is negative.

*Director:* Like your negative way in acting.

*Actor:* Yes.

*Professor:* So I teach my students to learn something positive from the negative of philosophy?

*Actor:* That's what you do.

*Director:* Is it possible to have too much negative?

*Actor:* You have to find the balance.

*Professor:* Director, do you find the balance?

*Director:* I do, but not in the way Actor suggests. My balance is like riding a bike. I have to keep moving forward and balance myself as I go.

*Actor:* You never stop?

*Director:* Well, I have to rest, eat, sleep, and so on. But on the whole? I never stop.

36

*Actor:* Just as I never stop seeking approval?

*Director:* Don't you?

*Actor:* No!

*Director:* Then what's your idea?

*Actor:* Maybe it's philosophy. After all, we have the negative in common. And there are plenty of bad ideas for me to attack.

*Director:* How will you attack them?

*Actor:* I'll just... attack!

*Director:* You'll say, "Your idea is bad!"

*Actor:* Well, I'll explain to them why it's bad.

*Director:* So will you think up your explanation in advance?

*Actor:* I suppose that's best.

*Director:* And to know how to explain, you have to know what they really think? I mean, so you can get to the heart of the matter?

*Actor:* Yes.

*Director:* How will you know what they really think?

*Actor:* I guess I have to ask them.

*Director:* And then you go home and think about what they said?

*Actor:* That's the way of it. But sometimes you already know what they think.

*Director:* How?

*Actor:* It's obvious.

*Director:* But how is it obvious?

*Actor:* If someone says the sky is never blue, I know what they think and I know they're wrong.

*Director:* So you'll just say, "The sky is often blue." And that will do it?

*Actor:* No, I'll have to show them the sky.

*Director:* And if they're blind?

*Actor:* Well, that's a different matter.

*Director:* Is it? They still have the wrong idea.

*Actor:* If I can't show them, I don't know how to correct their idea.

*Director:* And that's the first lesson of philosophy.

*Actor:* So what do we do? Avoid the blind?

*Director:* We avoid teaching the blind to see.

*Actor:* Because they'll never see.

*Director:* Well, medical technology might make us change this example one day—but yes, they'll never see.

*Actor:* How can we tell if someone is blind when it comes to ideas?

*Director:* We talk to them.

*Actor:* And what do we look out for when we do?

*Director:* False opinions that are set like stone.

*Actor:* They'll never change their mind?

*Director:* Not from anything we might do.

*Actor:* So we're looking for some flexibility?

*Director:* We're looking for some doubt.

*Actor:* But only reasonable doubt.

*Professor:* Why do you stipulate that?

*Actor:* Because unreasonable doubt is a problem.

*Professor:* A good teacher can help you here.

*Actor:* How?

*Professor:* By showing the way through doubt to the true.

*Actor:* And by teaching to hold on to the true?

*Professor:* Of course. We all have to hold on to the true.

*Actor:* And you, Director, with all of philosophy's negative force—do you hold on to the true?

*Director:* With all my might.

### 37

*Actor:* Would you say that without the true to hold on to, there can be no philosophy?

*Director:* I would.

*Professor:* There's one important thing to mention, however.

*Actor:* What thing?

*Professor:* The negative can be true.

*Actor:* Of course it can. It's not snowing, for instance. That can be a negative truth.

*Professor:* Then you see why I say philosophy might hold on with all its might—to the negative.

*Actor:* Director?

*Director:* Yes, and either way—positive or negative—we need to take our bearings by truth.

*Actor:* And when we do we're ready to attack the false?

*Director:* I'd rather say we're ready to persuade those who take their bearings from the false to realign. But we have to be open.

*Actor:* What do you mean?

*Director:* We have to be open to the possibility that we have something to learn.

*Actor:* What we thought was false might be true?

*Director:* It's certainly possible. But there's something else we can learn. We can learn what's often connected with what.

*Actor:* What do you mean?

*Director:* Certain false ideas affect certain people's lives.

*Actor:* Of course they do. What's there to learn there?

*Director:* Maybe how to help. If I come to see that false idea X usually involves life problem Y, when I see Y in someone I know, I check and see if X is present.

*Actor:* And if X is present?

*Director:* I try to get them to see it's false.

*Actor:* That sounds good. But you can just ask the person if they believe X.

*Director:* True, but it helps to go into it with, excuse me, some idea.

*Actor:* Why?

*Director:* Ideas that affect our lives deeply are often closely held. We don't readily share them. If I can come into the conversation with an idea of their idea, it helps.

*Actor:* Ideas of ideas. Do you take it further?

*Director:* Ideas of ideas of ideas? No, not really. It gets too confused.

*Professor:* It gets too deep. And if we go too deep, we might drown.

*Actor:* So what are you, Professor, some sort of life guard?

*Professor:* Of sorts, yes. Some of my students are afraid of the water, and some dive in when they don't know how to swim.

*Actor:* What is swimming when it comes to ideas?

*Professor:* It will sound so simple.

*Actor:* Tell us.

*Professor:* You have to be willing to think new thoughts.

*Actor:* You mean you have to open your mind?

*Professor:* Yes. You have to weigh and consider and then decide.

*Actor:* Decide about the new idea.

*Professor:* Right. And you can't do what many do—decide before they've considered.

*Actor:* What does consideration involve?

*Professor:* The attempt to arrive at understanding.

*Actor:* Being fair minded?

*Professor:* Yes. But also critical minded. If you're both critical and fair, chances are you'll come to the truth.

*Actor:* Director, if a philosopher had to choose between being critical or fair, which would it be?

*Director:* Why separate the two? If you're not critical, you can't know what's fair.

*Actor:* And if you're not fair?

*Director:* Your criticism misses the mark.

### 38

*Actor:* And the mark is truth.

*Director:* The mark is truth.

*Actor:* Can you say more about the idea of fairness?

*Director:* It's a cousin of the idea of justice. You've heard people say, "You've done justice to it"?

*Actor:* I have. It means to give something the treatment it deserves.

*Director:* That's all I mean when I talk about being fair to an idea.

*Actor:* But people's conception of justice differs.

*Director:* That's why we argue over ideas.

*Actor:* I thought we argue because we're concerned with truth.

*Director:* Justice and truth are closely related.

*Actor:* How?

*Director:* We can't get at the truth unless we're just.

*Actor:* Say more.

*Director:* What do we mean when we talk about giving something the treatment it deserves?

*Actor:* We examine it thoroughly and report what we find.

*Director:* Can we know the full truth without a thorough examination?

*Actor:* Some things are obvious on their face.

*Director:* Then a superficial examination is enough?

*Actor:* A superficial examination might be just. But what if we go deeper? Might we be... unjust?

*Director:* Let's have an example.

*Actor:* Cruelty. It doesn't deserve more than a superficial account.

*Director:* Why?

*Actor:* Because that's all it takes to know it's bad.

*Director:* And if we go deeper, looking for an explanation, a full account?

*Actor:* We do an injustice to the victims.

*Director:* The victims deserve ignorance concerning the cruelty? I thought victims often want a reason why.

*Actor:* It depends on the victim.

*Director:* So doing justice depends on the frame of mind of those who were treated unjustly?

*Professor:* Yes. But, Director, what if some people deserve to be treated cruelly?

*Director:* We'd only know that if we do justice to them. But listen to us. How do we know if justice is done?

*Actor:* Justice is done when the best account wins.

*Director:* The best account? And who judges which account is best?

*Actor:* Those in power.

*Director:* So power and justice are related.

*Actor:* Of course they are. That's why justice is never done for the weak. Not unless they grow strong, or some of the strong come over to them.

*Director:* Can the idea of justice make you grow strong?

*Actor:* I think it can.

*Director:* What about the idea of injustice?

*Actor:* What about it?

*Director:* Can it make you grow weak?

*Actor:* I'm not sure. Yes, these ideas are opposite sides of the same coin. But I'm not sure.

*Director:* Do other ideas have opposite sides of the same coin?

*Actor:* Of course. But what idea do you have in mind?

*Director:* Love.

*Actor:* Hate is never as powerful as love, opposite side or not.

*Director:* Why not?

*Actor:* Because if it is—then the world ends.

### 39

*Director:* Can injustice bring about the end of the world?

*Actor:* It can.

*Director:* Are there other such world-ending ideas?

*Actor:* I'm not so sure it's the idea and not the fact.

*Professor:* Ideas lead to facts. But don't get rid of the ideas of hate and injustice.

*Actor:* Why not?

*Professor:* Because what happens if bad things are never deemed hateful or unjust? We would lack the mental leverage to overcome them. We need those ideas.

*Director:* And what about good things?

*Actor:* What about them?

*Director:* Do they need the idea of justice?

*Actor:* Why would they?

*Director:* To secure them in their place.

*Actor:* I suppose that makes some sense. But good things and justice don't necessarily go hand in hand.

*Director:* Why not?

*Actor:* A sunny day is good, but it's not just. A stormy day is bad, but it's not unjust.

*Director:* So good things and bad things don't necessarily have to do with justice or injustice.

*Actor:* They don't.

*Director:* So why do we need the ideas of justice and injustice? Why not just say something is good or bad?

*Actor:* That's a good question. There can be good and bad verdicts in court. There can be good or bad laws.

*Director:* And there can be good or bad treatments or accounts of ideas?

*Actor:* Certainly.

*Director:* So instead of saying we gave it a just treatment, we can say we gave it a good and thorough treatment, or something like that.

*Actor:* We can.

*Director:* Then why is justice such a powerful idea?

*Actor:* I don't know.

*Director:* Are we giving justice a bad treatment?

*Actor:* I don't think so.

*Director:* Which would you rather have? Goodness or justice?

*Actor:* Goodness.

*Director:* Why?

*Actor:* Because goodness can include the idea of justice and more.

*Director:* Can goodness include love?

*Actor:* Yes.

*Director:* So goodness is the all-powerful idea. Or is there an idea that's stronger?

*Actor:* None that I can see.

*Director:* What about the idea of strength itself?

*Actor:* Strength is good.

*Director:* But it can be put to bad use.

*Actor:* Of course. That's why with the idea of good we have the idea of bad.

*Director:* And bad ends the world. Well, Professor. What do you think? Can goodness do away with the need for justice?

*Professor:* It can, and we should jettison the unnecessary idea.

*Director:* Are we sure there's never a time when we need the idea of justice instead of the good?

*Professor:* Not that I'm aware of. I mean, we can say when laws are followed that's good—it's good to follow the law. When an innocent is acquitted, that's good. And so on and so on.

*Director:* What does justice have that goodness doesn't? Anything?

*Actor:* Revenge?

*Director:* Is it good to take revenge?

*Actor:* It feels wrong to say it, but I think the answer is yes.

*Professor:* So justice has nothing that goodness doesn't.

*Actor:* That's how it seems. But you know, Professor, I'd like to see you go a year in school without the idea of justice.

*Professor:* I would, too. So I'll take up the challenge.

### 40

*Director:* Don't students often want to talk about social justice?

*Professor:* They do. And so we'll talk about the social good.

*Director:* Is it really as simple as substituting 'good' for 'justice'?

*Professor:* I don't know. It might be. We'll have to see how it goes.

*Director:* That makes me wonder how closely linked words are with ideas. 'Good' is the word for the idea in our language. It differs in others. But is the idea of good the same?

*Actor:* I don't think it is. Words matter. And translations never do justice—are never very good, I mean.

*Professor:* There are no supra-language ideas? Ideas common to all?

*Actor:* I don't think there are. They may be similar, but language renders them different.

*Professor:* What about the universal language?

*Actor:* Love? Maybe that's the only exception.

*Professor:* But surely 'good' and 'bad' are known by all. It's bad if a crop fails, for instance.

*Actor:* Yes, but different languages suggest different reasons for the failure.

*Director:* What do you mean?

*Actor:* One language might suggest a supernatural force was at work. Another might see the failure as purely natural, something humans can overcome.

*Director:* Some languages are influenced by science while others aren't?

*Actor:* Yes. The influence comes from a certain way of thought supported by and supporting certain ideas.

*Director:* I'd like to know more about science. Tell us, can science be unjust?

*Actor:* I never thought about it before. I suppose it can, yes.

*Director:* How?

*Actor:* It could mistakenly interpret something as bad that is in fact good. Its assessment is unjust.

*Professor:* Its assessment is bad, bad science—not unjust.

*Actor:* Fair enough.

*Director:* Tell me, Actor. Are there really only two types of language in the world? The scientific and the unscientific?

*Actor:* I don't know.

*Director:* How can we know?

*Actor:* I guess we'd have to know quite clearly what ideas each language has.

*Professor:* And the quality of those ideas.

*Actor:* Yes. But you can't just say scientific ideas make for higher quality.

*Professor:* Why not?

*Actor:* Because that's an assumption. And it's a dangerous assumption because the influence of science is growing.

*Professor:* Yes, but isn't there resistance?

*Actor:* There is some, yes.

*Professor:* Why do you think that is?

*Actor:* I think it has something to do with the reason why there are different languages today.

*Director:* Can you say more?

*Actor:* There will always be people who want to break away, or keep away, from the norm. It's human nature.

*Professor:* Always? I'm not so sure.

*Actor:* Why not?

*Professor:* Because of the force of bad and good.

*Actor:* What do you mean?

*Professor:* Let's stick with the notion of breaking away. We can deal with keeping away another time.

*Actor:* That's fine. So what of good and bad?

*Professor:* The ideas it's-bad-to-break-away and it's-good-to-stay might get so strong that no one will ever break away.

*Actor:* You speak as if you never met young people.

*Professor:* And you speak as if you never met young people who are wise beyond their years. Such people don't break away—not usually, at least.

*Actor:* What makes them wise?

*Professor:* Their strong ideas of good and bad. Why, what do you think wisdom is?

*Actor:* Director, is that what wisdom is?

*Director:* I've never heard it put that way before. But my first impression is that it's true.

*Actor:* So philosophy, the love of wisdom, is love of strong ideas of good and bad?

*Director:* Don't you want to know what's good and bad? Don't you want to have a strong idea?

*Actor:* Of course I do. Does that make me a philosopher?

*Director:* You have philosophical leanings, tendencies.

*Actor:* Tendencies?

*Professor:* Yes, Actor. But you said something interesting, Director.

*Director:* Oh no. Did I?

*Professor:* You suggested that having a strong idea is to know. Did you mean it?

*Director:* I usually mean what I say. Do you think it's true?

*Professor:* Of course not. You might have a strong idea that's false. So you might think you know—but don't.

### 41

*Director:* Thank goodness you're here to correct me.

*Actor:* People are generally happy to think they know. It's comforting.

*Director:* But actually knowing is more comforting?

*Actor:* I'm not sure. Some knowledge is hard to bear.

*Director:* What knowledge?

*Actor:* Knowledge of the bad.

*Professor:* But then you know to keep away. What a comfort that is.

*Actor:* Then tell me what's bad so I can keep away.

*Professor:* It's bad when things aren't clear.

*Actor:* So I should keep away from the murky?

*Professor:* You should attempt to make the murky clear.

*Actor:* Always?

*Director:* No, not always.

*Professor:* What's this?

*Director:* We should make things clear for ourselves. But what if we come across someone wallowing in muck? Is it always good to clear things up for them?

*Professor:* Yes.

*Actor:* I'm not sure about that, Professor. Say more, Director. Maybe you have an example?

*Director:* Suppose someone is violent and unstable. And they've lived their life in murk and muck. Is it wise to approach them and clear it all up? 'Your life has been wasted in murk,' we'll say. 'Here, let me demonstrate how.'

*Actor:* That's no doubt a bad idea. Professor?

*Professor:* Director is in a hurry. With patience, over a long stretch of time, we can make things clear.

*Actor:* And in the meantime we could have used our time to encourage many others, instead of spending it all on this person—a person who might snap on us!

*Professor:* You exaggerate how much time this takes. If might be half an hour every other week. And as for the danger? Life involves risks. But those risks are less when we're patient.

*Director:* How do we know when to move forward? How do we know when to make things more clear? This assumes, of course, we know what's wrong, that we can see.

*Professor:* We have to know the signs. We lead these people gently and let them arrive on their own. When they arrive at one point, we're ready to start out for another. Slowly.

*Actor:* But we're leading them down a path toward the conclusion that they've wasted their lives. That's going to become more clear as we proceed. Why would they stay with us to reach this end? It doesn't make sense.

*Professor:* Maybe I'm biased in that I always think of young people. They have time to realize the error of their ways and make the change.

*Director:* We can always make the change. Can't we? Besides, who can really say what's been a waste for whom?

*Actor:* It's up to each of us to say.

*Director:* And it's good for each of us to have the final say.

*Professor:* But what if we're wrong?

*Actor:* How can we be wrong about the meaning of our life?

*Director:* What do you say to this? If your belief in the meaning of your life is strong, we leave you alone. But if you're unsure, we help you clear things up.

*Actor:* That's a reasonable approach. But you assume we can help.

*Director:* Well, we're not providing the answer. We're listening, and asking questions.

*Actor:* And the person in question will arrive at the answer on their own?

*Director:* Yes, I think that's best. Don't you?

*Actor:* I do.

*Director:* And when they have the answer, they'll be strong in their belief?

*Actor:* If the answer is clear, yes—they'll be strong.

## 42

*Director:* Can a life be dedicated to an idea?

*Professor:* We should all dedicate our lives to the idea of goodness.

*Director:* Of course. But does that always happen?

*Professor:* It doesn't.

*Director:* People dedicate their lives to—how shall we say it?—lesser ideas?

*Professor:* Yes.

*Actor:* Name a lesser idea.

*Professor:* Fame. Or success. Or....

*Actor:* Or what? What don't you want to say?

*Professor:* Family.

*Actor:* Many people dedicate their lives to family. It's a very serious thing.

*Professor:* Yes, but not everyone does. And some of those who do are in a bad way.

*Actor:* How so?

*Professor:* For one? They use family as a prop for ambition.

*Actor:* True, that's a problem. But I see a more general problem.

*Professor:* Oh? What?

*Actor:* Family takes the place of goodness.

*Director:* What does that mean?

*Actor:* Have you ever seen someone who is fully, exclusively, dedicated to the idea of family—and is miserable? Why do you think that happens?

*Professor:* Because there's no good. Misery always follows from the absence of good.

*Director:* So if you're dedicated to family, that family must be good?

*Actor:* Or certain members of it, at least.

*Director:* Is that part of making things clear? Knowing who's good?

*Actor:* Yes.

*Professor:* Ah, but who are we to judge?

*Actor:* Someone has to judge.

*Director:* Are you sure? Maybe we can live our life without judgment.

*Actor:* That's to head down stream with no way to steer.

*Professor:* So we judge and steer by our judgments.

*Actor:* Right. But we can do more. We can try to help the bad ones see.

*Director:* See that they're bad?

*Actor:* Don't you think they need to know?

*Director:* I'm not sure about this. It sounds like trouble.

*Actor:* Since when are you afraid of trouble?

*Director:* Have you heard of the nuclear family? Well, nuclear warfare is the most dreaded thing on earth. Of course I'm afraid.

*Actor:* But when called to fight that war, we must.

*Director:* Why must we?

*Actor:* Because we can't sacrifice ourselves to them!

*Director:* Them?

*Actor:* The rotten ones! To do so is bad, as bad as it gets.

*Director:* And without the idea of goodness, we can't know they're bad?

*Actor:* No, we can't.

*Director:* So the idea of goodness must be above the idea of family.

*Actor:* Yes.

*Director:* And if we know what's good, we'll know how to run our family well?

*Actor:* Of course.

*Director:* Can we run our family well if we don't know what's good?

*Actor:* How could we?

*Director:* So family is a subordinate idea.

*Actor:* Subordinate to the good, yes. But, Director, everything is subordinate to the good.

*Director:* And that's a wonderful thing.

### 43

*Professor:* Is philosophy subordinate to the good?

*Director:* Ah, you caught me!

*Actor:* Caught you in what?

*Director:* Philosophy has a special relationship with the good.

*Actor:* What relationship?

*Professor:* I'll tell you. Philosophy brings the good out and makes it clear for all to see.

*Actor:* And included in that are friendship and love?

*Professor:* Yes, philosophy makes clear who are our friends are and who we should love.

*Director:* But in speaking of love for friends and love for lovers, we have to be careful.

*Actor:* Why?

*Director:* Because love is a tricky thing.

*Actor:* There's nothing simpler!

*Director:* In a sense, but things complicate quickly. And I'll say something I can hardly believe I'll say. We need to have some belief in love, in order to sustain us.

*Professor:* Here is a philosopher proposing belief!

*Director:* Am I proposing? I'm just saying what happens.

*Actor:* Does it happen with you?

*Director:* Do I believe in love? I believe it's not good to let go, unless there's real reason.

*Actor:* But if you loved you would never let go.

*Director:* Ah, but love doesn't necessarily make you brave.

*Actor:* Brave? You have to be brave to love? Why?

*Director:* Because love terrifies at times.

*Actor:* You're teasing. But what would make you brave?

*Director:* Knowledge.

*Actor:* Then why not have knowledge of love?

*Director:* Because when I'm afraid I sometimes forget what I know. And then I'm left with poor old belief.

*Actor:* What about love makes you afraid?

*Director:* Many things. But mostly? The chance of losing my love.

*Actor:* Well, who's not afraid of that? But does poor old belief sustain you?

*Director:* I believe it must.

*Actor:* Professor, what do you say about all this?

*Professor:* I'd be willing to take it on faith to keep my love intact.

*Actor:* Why?

*Professor:* Because I have to remember there was a reason for love in the first place.

*Actor:* A good reason?

*Professor:* I don't know.

*Actor:* Then why sustain the love?

*Professor:* So I can find out.

*Actor:* Why do I get the sense you two are playing fast and loose with your reasons?

*Professor:* Maybe because you're slow and tight with yours?

*Actor:* You'd accuse an actor of that?

*Professor:* Why, are actors always fast and loose?

*Actor:* I'm not. But I wouldn't say I'm slow and tight.

*Professor:* What are you?

*Actor:* The happy mean.

*Director:* You're a sort of average?

*Actor:* No. I'm the truth. The one true way.

44

*Professor:* The one true way is the midpoint between two opposites? Gray is the one true way between black and white?

*Actor:* Well, you're making it sound ridiculous

*Professor:* Why is it ridiculous?

*Actor:* Because gray is... gray!

*Professor:* Gray is never clear?

*Actor:* By definition.

*Professor:* Well, if it's by definition....

*Actor:* You have some better definition of gray?

*Professor:* No, I'm content with gray as unclear. But so much life takes place in the gray.

*Actor:* We need to pull life out.

*Professor:* Into the black and white?

*Actor:* Yes, we need things to be more clear.

*Professor:* You want a yes or a no with nothing in-between.

*Actor:* What's wrong with that? That's what logic wants.

*Professor:* Good logic can handle the in-between.

*Actor:* Not in my experience.

*Professor:* Look at it this way. Suppose you refuse to see anything that's not black or white. That can be good. It often gets you what you want. But suppose you're very stubborn when someone tries to explain something to you, something delicate, something that requires you to open your mind all the way—something gray.

*Actor:* The gray isn't delicate. It's cloudy and unclear. And I don't care for the notion that to be open minded we have to embrace the gray. My mind is wide open—to black and white.

*Professor:* But sometimes it's useful to be open to the gray.

*Actor:* Sometimes it's useful to lie, cheat, and steal.

*Professor:* It's not the same thing.

*Actor:* But in my stubbornness I think it is.

*Director:* And sometimes it's useful to be stubborn.

*Actor:* It certainly is.

*Director:* And the useful is good.

*Actor:* Yes. And you know I don't really believe it's useful to lie, cheat, and steal.

*Director:* Because it's wrong?

*Actor:* Yes. And the wrong has no use.

*Director:* Is it wrong to be stubborn at times?

*Actor:* Yes, of course.

*Director:* When?

*Actor:* When we're wrong.

*Director:* So sometimes it's good to be stubborn, sometimes not.

*Professor:* In other words, it can be good to be not always the same.

*Director:* Yes. Although....

*Actor:* Although what?

*Director:* Tell me. If each day we wear different clothes, does that mean we're different?

*Actor:* Of course not. But are you saying stubbornness is like clothing?

*Director:* I am. We put it on or take it off depending on what's good. And I think all character traits are like clothing—when it comes to the good.

### 45

*Actor:* I'm not sure I like that notion. What does it say about character?

*Professor:* It says we form ourselves toward goodness.

*Actor:* But what if the good is always changing? What kind of character do we have then?

*Director:* Well, that's a big question. Does the idea of the good really change?

*Professor:* No, not the idea, not goodness itself.

*Actor:* So what does that mean?

*Professor:* To answer that we need to explore. How do you distinguish between the idea and the thing itself?

*Actor:* The idea is like a map. The thing itself is like the actual destination.

*Professor:* Is happiness the destination?

*Actor:* I think it should be, yes.

*Professor:* So if being stubborn makes you happy...

*Actor:* ...then be stubborn, and that's good.

*Professor:* Is happiness always good?

*Actor:* Happiness is always good.

*Professor:* Does goodness always make you happy?

*Actor:* I'm not sure.

*Professor:* Why not? What's an example?

*Actor:* It might be good to save a drowning man. But in pulling him out you injure him. He sues you for damages and wins in court. This wipes out your savings. Good?

*Professor:* I see what you mean. Is there any way we can say it was bad to save the drowning man?

*Actor:* I don't see how.

*Professor:* Then goodness doesn't always make you happy.

*Actor:* So if you have to choose between happiness and goodness?

*Professor:* Choose happiness. Because happiness is always good.

*Actor:* But I wouldn't feel good if I didn't save the drowning man.

*Professor:* You mean you wouldn't be happy?

*Actor:* Yes.

*Professor:* You have to feel good to be happy?

*Actor:* Of course you do. Do you really think you can feel bad and be happy?

*Professor:* No, I don't. But what if you feel neither good nor bad? Happy?

*Actor:* No, you need to feel good.

*Professor:* Because happiness is good? And like goes with like?

*Actor:* Professor, what are you driving at?

*Professor:* I'm just exploring with you. Director, does like always go with like?

*Director:* You're asking if I have any idea how to sever goodness from happiness?

*Actor:* Do you?

*Director:* Not and maintain common sense.

*Actor:* But that's just it. Does philosophy always deal in common sense?

*Director:* It examines common sense to make sure it makes sense.

*Actor:* Common sense makes sense or philosophy makes sense?

*Director:* Both. And it doesn't make much sense to keep happiness and goodness apart.

*Actor:* Then let's get rid of happiness the way we got rid of justice.

*Director:* So when we're happy we'll say we feel good.

*Actor:* Exactly. Professor, keep happiness out of your class.

*Professor:* I'll do the best I can. But I have a feeling happiness and justice will creep back in.

*Actor:* Why?

*Professor:* Why? Because that's what they do. But what else will we reduce to good and bad? Love?

*Actor:* Of course not.

*Professor:* But love makes you feel good.

*Actor:* Love also makes you feel bad—when it's not returned.

*Professor:* Then we can say I feel good toward my wife, for instance; or I feel bad toward my wife.

*Actor:* But you can feel good or bad without love. Love is something more.

*Director:* It's the attraction we spoke of.

*Actor:* Exactly.

*Professor:* But you're attracted to those who make you feel good. And you're repelled by those who make you feel bad.

*Actor:* No. Love is more than feeling good.

*Professor:* Why?

*Actor:* Because 'I love you' implies a promise.

*Professor:* What promise?

*Actor:* 'I will always love you.'

*Professor:* Love is a pledge?

*Actor:* Yes.

*Professor:* But what if you stop feeling love? This is a problem, Actor. If we say 'you make me feel good,' isn't that more honest? When you stop feeling good you say you no longer feel good.

*Actor:* Yes, but it's not so simple.

*Director:* You mean it's not black and white?

*Actor:* Look. In the course of a day I might feel good ten times and bad an equal number.

*Professor:* So you keep score?

*Actor:* No, you remember your love, your pledge, and you carry on.

*Professor:* In hopes the next day you'll feel good a hundred times and bad only once?

*Actor:* You exaggerate, but yes.

*Professor:* I prefer the makes-me-feel-good over love. I'll banish justice, happiness, and love from my class.

*Actor:* I'd love to see how long that lasts. You'll reduce your students to creatures that simply grunt with pleasure or pain once you're done. After all, if we can get rid of justice, happiness, and love—what can't we reduce?

### 46

*Professor:* If my students simply grunt, what does that make them?

*Actor:* Pigs.

*Professor:* How can they get beyond being pigs?

*Actor:* They can have ideas.

*Professor:* Pigs don't have ideas?

*Actor:* Of course not.

*Professor:* What good do ideas do?

*Actor:* They lift us above.

*Professor:* To a height from which we can see... what?

*Actor:* The future and past.

*Professor:* Pigs live only in the present?

*Actor:* Of course.

*Professor:* What do we find in the future and past?

*Actor:* In the past we find lessons.

*Professor:* And in the future?

*Actor:* Hopes.

*Professor:* Pigs neither learn lessons nor hope?

*Actor:* They don't. And I'm not speaking of actual pigs. For all I know they do learn and hope.

*Professor:* Okay. But do all ideas elevate?

*Actor:* That's a good point. We can have base ideas.

*Professor:* Do pigs have base ideas?

*Actor:* I suppose they might.

*Professor:* What's an example of a base idea?

*Actor:* That pleasure and pain is all there is.

*Professor:* Hmm. There are philosophies, hedonistic philosophies, that say pleasure and pain is all—and they're hardly base. They talk about higher pleasures, like pleasures of the mind, the pleasure of friendship, and so on. And for pain they talk about the pains of falling away from duty, from being untrue to yourself, and so on.

*Actor:* Well, that doesn't sound base. But there are certainly many people who are concerned with the baser pleasures and pains.

*Professor:* Yes, but is their concern the function of an idea?

*Actor:* Probably not.

*Professor:* And if they say, "Grunt—this is pleasure, this is good," are they talking about our sort of good?

*Actor:* No, they're not.

*Professor:* So there are two sorts of goodness?

*Actor:* Yes, high and low.

*Professor:* Is the low always bad?

*Actor:* No, not always.

*Professor:* What's something that's low?

*Actor:* A bodily process.

*Professor:* Name such a process.

*Actor:* Eating, and all that it involves.

*Professor:* But aren't there high culinary arts? Can't eating be refined?

*Actor:* True, you can slop something down or you can savor with delight.

*Professor:* Just as you can slurp cheap beer or sip tasty wine?

*Actor:* Yes, but we're making it sound like high and low is a function of money.

*Professor:* What's it a function of?

*Actor:* The thought that goes into the thing. Money can't help you there. You can be rich and slurp expensive wine like a pig. You can be poor and savor an inexpensive, flavorful meal cooked by an angel with care.

47

*Director:* And angels don't grunt with pleasure.

*Actor:* No, they express pleasure in carefully chosen words.

*Director:* Words that do justice to the food?

*Actor:* Good words, yes—fitting.

*Professor:* Some would say justice is the fitting. After all, the fitting is what something deserves. Fine food deserves fine words of praise. The words do justice to the food.

*Actor:* Then we can say the words are good. The good always fits.

*Director:* Are we really going to reduce the fitting to the good?

*Actor:* Yes. So there's no justice, or happiness, or love, or anything that fits at your school, Professor—only goodness.

*Director:* And badness. But weren't you the one concerned with simply grunting and squealing like pigs?

*Actor:* Yes, but I want to see where this goes.

*Director:* Then what else can we reduce?

*Actor:* I don't know. Maybe those are all of the basic ideas.

*Director:* What about true or false?

*Actor:* Good or bad.

*Director:* And the ideas of math?

*Actor:* Good or bad—even though most will be good.

*Director:* Professor?

*Professor:* How about power?

*Actor:* Power is good; weakness is bad. 'I have the power to do this' becomes 'I have the goodness to do this'.

*Professor:* That's a stretch, isn't it?

*Actor:* No more than anything else we've said today. And, really, wouldn't you rather say 'I have the goodness to do this' than 'I have the power'?

*Professor:* I don't know. But I'm losing track of what we'll reduce.

*Director:* We'd do well to keep track of what we can't reduce.

*Professor:* The idea of nothingness.

*Actor:* And its opposite, somethingness? Can we say somethingness is good and nothingness is bad?

*Director:* I don't think we can. There might be times when we welcome nothingness, though I'd be hard pressed to say when.

*Professor:* So somethingness and nothingness can't simply reduce to good and bad.

*Director:* That's how it seems.

*Actor:* I think Professor should call his course 'Nothing and the Good'.

*Professor:* You have a knack for naming. Director, what do you think?

*Director:* That name would attract me. But I've thought of something else we might not be able to reduce.

*Actor:* Oh? What?

*Director:* The idea of age—young and old. Neither are necessarily good or bad.

*Actor:* But we can say something or someone is of a good age, or a bad age.

*Professor:* But that doesn't tell us anything about the age.

*Actor:* Well, we can say the same about temperature—hot or cold. Neither is necessarily good or bad.

*Director:* Yes, and then there's rough or smooth; tall or short; narrow or wide. I think we could go on.

*Actor:* I'm sure we could.

*Professor:* So it's only certain ideas that can be reduced. And maybe we don't have them all. But I think we've got the idea—of reduction, that is.

*Director:* What are they once again?

*Professor:* Justice, happiness, love, the fitting. And I think we can include pleasure and pain—one is good and the other is bad. So we can say 'this feels good' and 'this feels bad' .

*Actor:* Okay, that's fine. Justice, happiness, love, the fitting, pleasure. All are banished from your class.

*Director:* Yes, and we mentioned truth and power. Two plus two is four—that's good. And I'm good enough to lift this heavy weight.

*Professor:* Fine. Justice, happiness, love, the fitting, pleasure, truth, power. All can be reduced. All are either good, as in justice is good; or they are bad, as in injustice is bad.

### 48

*Director:* What's the advantage of banishing these ideas from class?

*Professor:* It will force us to think in a new way. We'll make discoveries.

*Actor:* And we'll be rid of the baggage the reduced ideas carried.

*Director:* What's an example of baggage?

*Actor:* Some people have hang-ups with the idea of pleasure. They think it's bad. If we call it goodness, it's easier to think of it as good.

*Director:* I see. Is it the same with power?

*Actor:* Yes, some people have a hard time thinking of power as good. But if we call it goodness....

*Director:* So we're engaged in some sort of propaganda?

*Actor:* No. Pleasure and power are good. It's not propaganda.

*Director:* But following our lead, anyone could roll any idea into the idea of goodness.

*Actor:* Not persuasively.

*Director:* I don't know. Sometimes people are persuaded of strange things.

*Professor:* By charismatic speakers.

*Actor:* Why are you two looking at me?

*Professor:* Have you ever heard the saying 'don't give them any ideas'?

*Actor:* Yes.

*Professor:* It's directed at people like you.

*Actor:* Why, because I play charismatics on screen?

*Professor:* Yes, and it's not a far step from playing a charismatic in real life.

*Actor:* I have no interest in that.

*Professor:* You've had no opportunity in that—yet.

*Actor:* What's an idea I might give?

*Professor:* A reduction. Unity is good; division is bad.

*Actor:* But that's true. Isn't it?

*Professor:* Well, let's ask—unity in what?

*Actor:* The people.

*Professor:* What unifies them?

*Actor:* Love for one another.

*Professor:* What if they're unified in hate for others?

*Actor:* That wouldn't be good.

*Professor:* So unity isn't always good.

*Actor:* No, it's not.

*Professor:* To tell them it's always good is to lie.

*Actor:* Of course.

*Professor:* And to tell them they're united in love when they're really united in hate?

*Actor:* That's a very big lie, I think.

*Professor:* Now what about our reduction of love into goodness and hate into badness?

*Actor:* What about it? The people should unite in goodness not badness.

*Professor:* What if they think by goodness you mean pleasure, and by badness you mean pain—and they find pleasure in hate and pain in love?

*Actor:* Well, that's a problem.

*Director:* A big enough problem that we need separate ideas of goodness and pleasure?

*Actor:* I think it is and we do.

*Director:* So we're reversing one of our reductions.

*Actor:* We have to.

*Director:* And what about our reduction of justice into goodness? Does that stay intact?

*Actor:* It does. Justice is always good.

*Director:* So justice as the good makes for a sound idea?

*Actor:* With no doubt.

### 49

*Director:* But pleasure and the good together falls apart.

*Actor:* Right, it doesn't make for a sound idea.

*Director:* Professor, how will you know sound ideas in your class?

*Professor:* The students and I will put them to the test.

*Actor:* And if what you thought was sound falls apart?

*Professor:* We simply keep looking for the sound.

*Director:* Hmm. I wonder if our critique of what seemed sound was sound.

*Actor:* What do you mean?

*Director:* Our idea of pleasure reduced to the good fell apart by pulling just one thread—finding pleasure in hate. Finding the good in the bad. But we didn't ask if hate can truly be a pleasure.

*Actor:* Can it?

*Director:* I'm not sure. Maybe there are different types of pleasure?

*Actor:* What do you mean?

*Director:* When I go for a swim, for instance, I feel pleasure. Is hate a pleasure like that?

*Actor:* Of course not.

*Director:* When my beloved says 'I love you', I feel pleasure. Is hate a pleasure like that?

*Actor:* No.

*Director:* When I sip a fine wine, I feel pleasure. Is hate a pleasure like that?

*Actor:* It... might be.

*Director:* How so?

*Actor:* I don't know. It just strikes me as potentially similar. I mean, can't you be drunk on hate?

*Director:* Yes, you can. But is drunkenness a pleasure?

*Actor:* Many would say it is.

*Professor:* I don't think it is. Feeling a little loose is a pleasure. But to be out and out drunk? To lose control? No, that's no pleasure.

*Director:* It's a pleasure to be in control?

*Professor:* Of course it is. Ask anyone who's not in control for reasons other than wine.

*Actor:* I think Professor has a point.

*Director:* Yes, he does. So what about sipping wine and hate?

*Professor:* Hate is a poison. Is it a pleasure to sip at poison?

*Actor:* I don't know. It might be.

*Professor:* It's a pleasure poison your body? Poison harms. Is harm a pleasure?

*Actor:* I want to say no.

*Professor:* Then sipping wine and hate are nothing alike.

*Actor:* And then things haven't fallen apart.

*Director:* What do we say to those who say they take pleasure in injustice, and the false, and so on?

*Professor:* We say they have no idea what pleasure is.

50

*Actor:* How can someone not know pleasure?

*Professor:* They never experienced it before.

*Actor:* How is that possible?

*Professor:* A correction. They never experienced pure goodness in pleasure before.

*Director:* Why not?

*Professor:* Because their feelings are all tangled up. And so they don't believe pure goodness exists.

*Director:* They think those who claim to know such goodness lie?

*Professor:* Or are fools that don't know the truth.

*Director:* What is the truth for these tangled up souls?

*Professor:* Nothing but nothingness and power. And power is the only thing that keeps the nothing away.

*Actor:* But then they do know pure good, the pure good of power.

*Professor:* True, in a way. But they don't think of power as good. Power is power—the only thing worth having.

*Director:* But can it cut through the tangle?

*Professor:* Yes. It's the only thing that lets them breathe.

*Actor:* So the tangle is like tight bands around the chest?

*Director:* And the struggle for power is more than ambition. It's a desperate struggle for life.

*Actor:* I think that describes it well.

*Director:* And when you achieve power, you don't feel pleasure—you feel relief.

*Actor:* There's a pleasure in relief. But you're basically right.

*Professor:* But it's good to be able to breathe.

*Actor:* Of course. But you can find better, more reliable ways to respire.

*Director:* So though we find good, we should seek better?

*Professor:* Not always. Sometimes people aren't happy with the good they have because they have the nagging belief there's something better.

*Director:* Then we should be content with our good unless there's clear evidence of a better way. And what about our hard-to-breathe friends? How do they know there's better?

*Actor:* Someone has to show them.

*Director:* And what does that involve?

*Actor:* Untangling the feelings.

*Director:* But I thought they would cut the tangle. Isn't that easier?

*Actor:* Easier, sure. But then you have to tie what you cut back together.

*Professor:* And by nature feelings aren't tied.

*Director:* What does that mean? There can be no natural feeling after a cut?

*Actor:* I think we've reached the limit of the metaphor.

*Director:* Then let's ask this. What's the idea of a metaphor?

*Actor:* I don't know. I suppose it's talking about something by talking about something else. Why?

*Director:* It occurred to me. Metaphors can be good or bad—good when they're apt, bad when they're not.

*Actor:* You don't think the tangle is a good metaphor?

*Director:* No, I think it is. That's why I think we haven't reached its limit.

*Actor:* Okay. Then let's get back to what we were saying. No, I don't think there's the same sort of natural feeling after the cut and repair.

*Director:* Is it for this reason? Some repairs are stronger than the original state.

*Actor:* That's true. But I wasn't thinking of that. I was thinking the person will always have scars.

*Director:* What's wrong with scars?

*Actor:* You might not feel your feelings very well.

*Director:* Because the scars interfere? What happens if you don't feel your feelings very well?

*Actor:* You might get the wrong idea about them.

*Director:* You might think good is bad and bad is good?

*Actor:* I think you might.

*Director:* So you can't trust your feelings?

*Actor:* I don't like to say it, but....

*Director:* Then what can you trust?

*Professor:* You can trust reason—your mind.

*Actor:* That's a dangerous thing, putting reason above feeling.

*Professor:* Why?

*Actor:* Because reason is rooted in feeling.

*Professor:* That's really your idea of reason?

*Actor:* Do you think it's wrong?

*Professor:* When things go well, reason and feeling are one. Good feeling brings on good reason; and good reason brings on good feeling.

*Director:* Good feeling really brings on good reason?

*Professor:* Why wouldn't it?

*Director:* When we're feeling good we might feel no need to reason.

*Actor:* Director has a point. And that makes me wonder. Does bad feeling bring on bad reason?

*Professor:* What do you think?

*Actor:* When we're feeling bad we need good reason more than ever.

*Director:* I think that makes sense. But now there's something I'm wondering. Is bad reason really reason?

*Professor:* No, it's not.

*Actor:* What is it?

*Professor:* Nonsense.

*Actor:* So we speak reason or not. There is no good or bad reason.

*Professor:* Yes, that's right.

*Actor:* Then reason can't be reduced.

### 51

*Director:* So what do we have? Goodness, nothingness, and reason. The irreducibles.

*Actor:* Are you forgetting age?

*Director:* So I am.

*Actor:* And what about temperature? And texture? And height and width?

*Professor:* Yes, and what about color? You can't reduce blue to good or bad.

*Director:* Look how forgetful I am! And how my imagination wasn't strong enough to think of color before! Thank goodness for friends like you.

*Actor:* So what do we have?

*Director:* Something more to discuss. Memory and imagination.

*Actor:* Memory is always good.

*Director:* My memory isn't always good.

*Actor:* That's so when you can't remember.

*Director:* Is it the same with imagination? Imagination is always good? And it's bad when you don't have it?

*Actor:* I think they're both like reason. Memory exists or it doesn't; imagination exists or it doesn't. Both memory and imagination can be used for good or ill.

*Director:* Is 'ill' the same as 'bad'?

*Actor:* Yes, why?

*Director:* Just checking to be sure. But what happens when we remember our imaginings?

*Actor:* What do you mean?

*Director:* Suppose you have a very active imagination, and you remember all the things you imagine, but not the outside world so much.

*Actor:* Well, that's obviously very bad.

*Director:* Why?

*Actor:* Because you're out of touch!

*Director:* Out of touch with what?

*Actor:* The world!

*Professor:* Is the world so good we should always be in touch?

*Actor:* Maybe not always. But most of the time, certainly.

*Professor:* What do we get from keeping in touch?

*Actor:* You can't survive if you don't.

*Professor:* So we have no choice but to keep in touch?

*Actor:* Yes.

*Professor:* That means the person with the most active imagination, one who lives in imagination, is somehow in touch—or else they couldn't survive. They have no choice.

*Actor:* When you put it like that I have to modify my answer. We don't have no-choice-but-to-keep-in-touch. Some of us get lost.

*Director:* Because we're very ill?

*Actor:* Yes, very ill indeed.

*Director:* So there's good imagination and bad imagination? Good imagination is somehow in touch; bad imagination is lost.

*Actor:* Right.

*Director:* When you act, Actor, do you use your imagination?

*Actor:* Of course I do. I imagine what my character would do.

*Director:* How do you stay in touch?

*Actor:* Me? My imagination pleases the audience.

*Director:* And if it didn't? You'd be out of touch?

*Actor:* I suppose I would.

*Director:* So staying in touch means to please.

*Actor:* There's truth in that.

*Director:* And people are in insane asylums because they don't please.

*Actor:* No, it's because they're sick.

*Director:* But they're not in touch, meaning they don't please.

*Actor:* Okay, okay. The insane don't please.

*Director:* The sick don't please.

*Actor:* Now you're being ridiculous.

*Director:* I am? Do the sick please?

*Actor:* The non-insane sick can please.

*Director:* And sometimes the insane sick can please?

*Actor:* Fair enough. Yes.

*Director:* And sometimes the non-insane sick don't please?

*Actor:* Sometimes they don't please.

*Director:* But, no matter, those who aren't in touch don't please.

*Actor:* Agreed.

## 52

*Director:* Pleasure is good.

*Actor:* Pleasure is good.

*Director:* To please is good.

*Actor:* To please is good.

*Director:* Not to please is bad.

*Actor:* I won't go along with that.

*Director:* Why not?

*Actor:* You know very well. Sometimes it's good not to please.

*Director:* Sometimes it's good to be out of touch?

*Actor:* Not every pleasing act is in touch.

*Director:* Ah. In touch with what?

*Actor:* The truth.

*Director:* Sometimes there's no pleasure in truth?

*Actor:* Of course.

*Director:* But truth is good. Pleasure is good.

*Actor:* Maybe we're finding the limit of good.

*Professor:* That sounds like a wonderful seminar name—The Limit of Good. Do you mind if I borrow it?

*Director:* But shouldn't we take pleasure in truth? If all is as it should be, if all is well—there will be pleasure in each and every truth.

*Professor:* I want you in the seminar, Director.

*Director:* Well, Actor? What do you say? Shouldn't we take pleasure in truth?

*Actor:* You've introduced another idea.

*Director:* Oh no! What have I done? What idea?

*Actor:* The idea of should.

*Director:* Should aligns with good.

*Actor:* Should should align with good.

*Director:* Sometime should aligns with bad?

*Actor:* Of course it does.

*Director:* But only when should is misused.

*Actor:* Well, yes. But it's still a should nonetheless.

*Director:* So we have good should and bad should. What is should?

*Actor:* It implies a duty.

*Director:* What is duty?

*Actor:* Something you're obliged to do.

*Director:* What is obligation?

*Actor:* A thing that has moral force.

*Director:* Can we say moral power? I don't want to get bogged down in discussing the difference between power and force.

*Actor:* Sure, we can say that. An obligation is a thing that has moral power.

*Director:* A good priest has moral power. Is the priest an obligation?

*Actor:* No, but a good priest reminds us of our obligations.

*Director:* Where do these obligations come from? Does the priest just make them up?

*Actor:* Sometimes, yes. Sometimes he or she gets them from others.

*Director:* Bishops and such?

*Actor:* And even the congregation.

*Director:* When hedonist philosophers tell me I should seek pleasure, what are they saying?

*Actor:* You have an obligation to yourself.

*Director:* A moral obligation to seek pleasure?

*Actor:* Yes. Why, you don't like that?

*Director:* Why does the obligation have to be moral?

*Actor:* Because the philosophers said 'should'.

*Director:* So if the philosophers say, "If you want to be good, then seek pleasure," the moral is all but erased?

*Actor:* There's nothing moral in if/then statements.

*Director:* Then there's nothing moral in logic.

*Actor:* Logic is like reason, if it's not reason whole. It is or it isn't. The moral doesn't enter into the equation.

*Professor:* Of course the moral enters into the equation.

*Actor:* Yes, but it's on an equal footing with any other term.

*Director:* Can we say the moral is or it isn't?

*Actor:* We can certainly say should is or it isn't.

*Director:* But should is moral and the moral is should.

*Professor:* How profound we three are. We discovered that 'should' is moral.

*Actor:* But is that what 'moral' is? The moral is right conduct.

*Professor:* What is 'right'?

*Actor:* Right leads to good.

*Professor:* I'll buy that. Director?

*Director:* I'm not sure I have the funds for such a large purchase.

*Actor:* What's large about right leading to good?

*Director:* Don't you know? You were the one who said there's good should and bad. Just the same, there's good right and bad right.

*Actor:* Okay. Good right leads to good; bad right leads to bad.

*Professor:* How do we know when we have the good or bad version?

*Actor:* We'll feel good.

*Professor:* So it's always right to do what feels good?

*Actor:* No, we can't say that.

*Director:* Why not?

*Actor:* Because it might feel good sleep late and miss work. But it's not good to miss work.

*Professor:* Maybe it is.

*Actor:* Maybe it is. But in my experience, it isn't.

### 53

*Director:* There's something about the future here, future good.

*Professor:* Yes, I've noticed that. There's a tradeoff.

*Actor:* What are you two talking about?

*Professor:* A sacrifice of present good for future good. Or, a sacrifice of lesser good for greater good.

*Actor:* The lesser good of sleep for the greater good of my acting career.

*Professor:* Yes. Does sleep make you happy?

*Actor:* It does.

*Professor:* Does your career?

*Actor:* Mostly.

*Professor:* So you trade a certain good for a somewhat ambiguous good.

*Actor:* I have to earn a living. There's nothing ambiguous in that. In fact, my career allowed me to buy my bed, on which I sleep. So you can say I have my priorities straight.

*Professor:* One good depends on another.

*Actor:* Of course.

*Professor:* Can we say all the goods depend on the greatest good?

*Actor:* What's the greatest good?

*Professor:* Clear thought. What do you think?

*Actor:* Maybe.

*Professor:* Why only maybe? What else can provide for all our needs? You can't say it's money because without clear thought you can't use your money well. What else could the greatest good be?

*Actor:* Love?

*Professor:* Yes, love. But with love you have to interact with your love. You have to interact well. What allows you to do that but clear thought?

*Actor:* There's nothing clear thought can't help you do well?

*Professor:* Nothing. Director, are we mistaken?

*Director:* Not to my thinking, no.

*Actor:* But what is thought? Logical reasoning?

*Professor:* What else would it be?

*Actor:* Feelings.

*Professor:* Feelings are facts to be reasoned upon.

*Director:* But feelings change.

*Professor:* So do other facts.

*Director:* So we must constantly reason.

*Professor:* We must constantly think.

*Actor:* But sometimes we need to rest.

*Professor:* True, but we never put our reason to sleep.

*Actor:* Our reason idles?

*Professor:* Yes, and is ready at a moment's notice to engage.

*Actor:* And is the idea that reason always finds the good?

*Professor:* Reason should be like a compass where north is the good.

*Director:* True north or magnetic north?

*Professor:* It doesn't matter. There is only one good.

*Actor:* But everyone's good differs. What's good for me might not be good for you.

*Director:* He has a point, you know.

*Professor:* We each have our own north.

*Actor:* And that's why there's strife in the world.

*Professor:* There's strife because we don't all travel straight.

*Director:* Are you saying there'd be harmony if only we all thought clear thoughts and acted on them?

*Professor:* Maybe not harmony, but there would be no strife. We wouldn't get in each other's way.

*Actor:* It's a sign of a lack of thought to block another's way?

*Professor:* Yes.

*Actor:* But how can you prove that?

*Professor:* If you're busy blocking you're not following your own way.

*Actor:* What if your way is to block?

*Director:* That's the question, isn't it? Does each of us have a good way? Or are some proper ways bad?

*Actor:* In other words, are some people inherently good and some inherently bad?

*Director:* That's the question. And I'm not sure we can know the answer. I think we can only posit an idea. Either all human beings are good, but some can't find their way; or some human beings are bad, and that's their way.

*Professor:* Or all human beings are bad, and some pretend to be good.

*Director:* So which is it for you, Actor?

*Actor:* I'd rather have no idea here—and take it as it comes.

## 54

*Professor:* Why?

*Actor:* Because I like to help where I can. And it doesn't matter to me if someone is good, bad, or whatever.

*Director:* How do you help?

*Actor:* If someone is blocking, I help get them out of the way.

*Director:* And if someone can't find their north?

*Actor:* I help them see.

*Director:* You really like to help?

*Actor:* I really do.

*Director:* Is it good to do what we really like?

*Actor:* There's nothing finer.

*Professor:* Some people like to torture animals.

*Actor:* Well, that's never good.

*Director:* But do you really think they like it?

*Actor:* They absolutely do—as much as anyone likes anything at all.

*Director:* So some people like the bad, torture.

*Actor:* Yes.

*Director:* If you like the bad, are you bad?

*Actor:* You are at the time.

*Director:* What do you mean?

*Actor:* People can reform.

*Director:* They come to like good things?

*Actor:* They come to regret and hate the bad.

*Professor:* Director, do you believe people can reform?

*Director:* It's not a matter of belief. I've seen it happen.

*Professor:* But maybe they were good, went bad, then became good once more?

*Director:* That's possible. Or maybe they were bad, died inside, and then became good.

*Actor:* And none of that matters. The point is that they stop the torture.

*Professor:* What matters are results. But that makes me wonder. Can we achieve good results in a way that's bad?

*Actor:* I think we can.

*Professor:* What's an example?

*Actor:* You steal money in order to fund an animal sanctuary.

*Professor:* But would someone do that?

*Actor:* Why not? Because if you're good to animals you're good to people, too? It doesn't always work that way, though we know it often does.

*Professor:* But then the results aren't good—they're mixed. Good for the animals, bad for the people.

*Actor:* So what's the idea? We need good ends for all?

*Director:* We've come back to war.

*Actor:* How so?

*Director:* Can we ever win a war with good ends for all, enemies included? Or would you say enemies aren't 'all'?

*Actor:* No, they're 'all'. You have a point.

*Director:* So what are we to think? Is winning a war not a good end?

*Actor:* Of course winning a war is good.

*Director:* Good for all?

*Actor:* The bad deserve to lose.

*Director:* And it's good to get what you deserve.

*Actor:* Of course.

*Director:* So the ends for all are good.

*Actor:* Assuming the good win the war.

*Director:* Now what about means?

*Actor:* What about them?

*Director:* How do we define a good means?

*Professor:* Many would say an effective means is good. Effectiveness makes for good.

*Actor:* Well, that opens the door to using whatever means necessary to achieve the desired end—'bad' means included.

*Director:* The desired end. That's really it, isn't it? That's what counts.

*Actor:* Why do you say that?

*Director:* Because when people really want something, they'll often do what it takes—no matter what it takes.

*Actor:* True. So what are you getting at?

*Director:* What if we could persuade people to want what we want them to want?

*Actor:* I'm not following.

*Director:* We want them to want an end that would require good means.

*Actor:* And the end is an idea?

*Director:* The idea is the end.

## 55

*Actor:* Do you know of an idea like this?

*Director:* No. But it makes sense that there could be one, doesn't it?

*Actor:* I think it does.

*Professor:* Yes, but you know the difficulty, don't you?

*Actor:* What difficulty?

*Professor:* Don't they say each end is a beginning?

*Actor:* They do.

*Professor:* Can we control what beginning will come of our end?

*Actor:* Not always.

*Professor:* I'd say it's more than 'not always'. I'd say we can't. I'd say it's impossible to control what this beginning will be.

*Actor:* So bad might come of our good.

*Professor:* Yes.

*Actor:* But we can't worry about what we can't control.

*Director:* That's a liberating view.

*Actor:* It is. It's impossible to know all that follows from everything we do. We have to draw the line at a certain point. And that's why we call something an end—we draw a line.

*Director:* And if we draw no line?

*Actor:* We have no end? We only have means?

*Director:* Good means.

*Actor:* Good means, sure. But I don't know, Director. We'd have no purpose in life.

*Director:* No purpose but living from good means to good means? Is that so bad?

*Actor:* 'Means' implies 'end'. Without an end you have no means. And then what do you have? Nothing.

*Director:* Well, we don't want that. But let's get back to the point. Good means for a good end is not impossible.

*Actor:* I agree. Professor?

*Professor:* I think we can sell the idea of a good end that requires good means.

*Actor:* And when we say 'requires', we mean it as a matter of necessity.

*Professor:* Yes.

*Director:* If only we knew an end like this. But sometimes pointing out possibilities is enough.

*Actor:* How so?

*Director:* Someone smarter than us might come along and figure it out.

*Professor:* That happens with my students. I give them an idea and they set to work—and arrive at places I never would have dreamed.

*Director:* Some people are truly motivated this way, by ideas. Aren't you, Actor? I mean, look at your idea of acting.

*Actor:* Yes, of course. I'm motivated by that idea. And you?

*Director:* I'm motivated by every idea.

*Actor:* Every idea? That can't be.

*Director:* But it's true! I want to know more about every idea I encounter.

*Actor:* Why?

*Director:* It's my good. Just like acting is your good.

*Actor:* And you, Professor?

*Professor:* I'm motivated by my students' ideas. The ones they have and the ones they'll acquire.

*Actor:* Acquire by virtue of your teaching?

*Professor:* By virtue of the class as a whole. We all teach each other. And when we learn, new vistas open toward better ideas.

*Actor:* Do students ever fail to take up better ideas when they see them?

*Professor:* Yes, unfortunately.

*Actor:* What holds them back?

*Professor:* Laziness, fear, loyalty.

*Actor:* How so laziness?

*Professor:* A new idea requires you to think many things through.

*Actor:* And fear?

*Professor:* Change is scary. What can I say?

*Actor:* And what about loyalty?

*Professor:* Some are loyal to certain ideas. If a better idea comes along, they have a hard time.

*Director:* Not if the better idea serves the same end as those certain ideas.

*Professor:* If the better idea is a means? Yes, that's true.

*Actor:* That's the best way to change ideas. To keep the end but switch out the means.

*Director:* And what's the best way to change an end?

*Actor:* You have to find a better end, one more appealing.

*Director:* And when you do, you change all the ideas that served as means, to have them suit the new end?

*Actor:* Yes. But that's a great shock.

*Director:* So what do we do?

*Actor:* Change the end-idea, then change the means-ideas one at a time.

## 56

*Director:* Hmm. Let's get back to something. Is it good to be lazy?

*Actor:* No, of course not.

*Director:* Is it good to be afraid?

*Actor:* No.

*Director:* Is it good to be loyal?

*Actor:* Yes, usually.

*Director:* Usually?

*Actor:* It's good to be loyal to good things, and bad to be loyal to the bad.

*Professor:* If it's so simple, why are so many people loyal to the bad?

*Actor:* It's all they know.

*Director:* And if they get to know the good?

*Actor:* They'll want to switch their loyalty.

*Director:* If the good and bad are people, is this an easy switch?

*Actor:* No, and it can be dangerous.

*Director:* Does that mean they should take things slowly?

*Actor:* Far from it. It means it's safest to make the switch all at once.

*Director:* Do they prepare for the switch or do it all on a whim?

*Actor:* They certainly prepare. You have to look before you leap. But when you're ready, you move as fast as you can.

*Director:* Why are half measures so bad here?

*Actor:* When you're halfway in anything, it's a drain. So you want to minimize the halfness. The problem here is if you're drained and dealing with the bad, they have you at a disadvantage. And they'll resent your treating with the good. That only makes it worse.

*Director:* I see. And if we're not talking about people but ideas?

*Actor:* It's the same.

*Director:* But not as dangerous?

*Actor:* No, it's dangerous. Dangerous in your mind.

*Director:* You mean you might have a breakdown.

*Actor:* Yes. A divided mind is never good.

*Director:* So we can't hold two opposed ideas in mind?

*Actor:* We can, as an experiment. But you can't live by two opposed ideas. Not for long, at least.

*Director:* But I think there are people with chronically opposed ideas.

*Actor:* Sure, but they're not well.

*Director:* How long do you think they can carry on?

*Actor:* How long can someone be sick? All their life. It's very sad.

*Director:* What can we do to help?

*Actor:* Show them that either one or both ideas are bad.

*Director:* How will we know they're bad?

*Actor:* From our own experience of life.

*Director:* The sick person has experience of life. What makes ours better?

*Actor:* We're not sick.

*Director:* How do we know?

*Actor:* Director, we all know when we're well or not.

*Director:* But some won't admit when they're not feeling well. Why?

*Professor:* I'll tell you why. You might suspect you're not well because of a bad idea. If you admit you're not well, it might lead someone to question your bad idea. If someone questions your bad idea, you might have to do something about your idea. That's where loyalty, fear, and laziness come in.

*Actor:* The loyal have the hardest time.

*Director:* Why?

*Actor:* Everyone fears when changing ideas. Everyone feels lazy in doing what must be done to bring themselves in line. But only the loyal have to deal with loyalty, too.

*Professor:* The loyal have more to overcome.

*Actor:* Exactly. So it's hardest on them. And they deserve the most credit.

57

*Director:* Then take it easy on the loyal in class, Professor.

*Professor:* You don't think I need to be tough?

*Actor:* You need to be firm. But you have to be gentle and patient with them. The best of them will always come around. It just might not happen while they're students.

*Director:* When they come around, how will they treat their former peers, those still loyal to the bad people or ideas?

*Actor:* First they'll need time, lots of time, in their new place in the world. They need to grow strong.

*Professor:* And when they have?

*Actor:* They'll be like you were to them—gentle, firm, and patient.

*Director:* And if they don't see results?

*Actor:* They have to trust they're doing the best they can, and that one day their peers might come around, too.

*Director:* I don't know, Actor. I think they might be impatient.

*Actor:* Why?

*Director:* Because they feel they need to make up for lost time.

*Actor:* You have to save so many souls in order to save your own?

*Director:* Yes, something like that. And since you mention soul, there's a problem some of the loyal will have.

*Actor:* What problem?

*Director:* Switching ideas seems like selling their soul.

*Actor:* How does someone get over that?

*Professor:* They need to see soul on the other side, the new side.

*Actor:* See or feel?

*Professor:* Sometimes to see is to feel.

*Actor:* Feeling soul isn't always enough.

*Director:* What more do they need?

*Actor:* Knowledge.

*Professor:* Of what?

*Actor:* You have to know you're not the only one.

*Director:* The only one?

*Actor:* Who ever crossed over.

*Professor:* But these things happen all the time.

*Actor:* Not in one's own life they don't.

*Director:* Yes. And what if you are the only one?

*Professor:* That's a dangerous thought, Director. There are always others who've changed sides when it comes to ideas.

*Actor:* But what if they're not many? And what if they can't be reached?

*Professor:* You have to make the effort to find them.

*Actor:* And do what? Say, "I heard you switched sides. I'm thinking of switching, too"?

*Professor:* If you switched sides, and someone in all honesty said that to you, wouldn't you go out of your way to help?

*Actor:* I would. Director?

*Director:* I'd feel compelled, I think.

*Actor:* Have either of you switched sides?

*Professor:* I have. But that's all I'll say.

*Actor:* And you, Director?

*Director:* I was never on a side to switch.

*Actor:* Never on a side? How is that possible? What about the idea of philosophy? Did you always side there?

*Director:* Didn't we say something about philosophy being the idea of having no ideas?

*Actor:* So philosophy is a paradox? Or is it the idea of having only one idea?

*Professor:* Don't let him distract us, Actor. We want to know if there are those on a side opposed to philosophy. If so, then philosophy is on the other side.

*Director:* It would be foolish to assert no one is opposed to philosophy. So, yes, I'm on the other side.

*Actor:* Then you know the question. Was there a time when you weren't?

*Director:* When I was opposed to philosophy? No.

*Actor:* So you were always on philosophy's side?

*Director:* Is anyone born a philosopher and thus established on philosophy's side? Professor?

*Professor:* No one is born a philosopher. We all become one. We choose to take a side. And we're obliged to help others join us.

*Actor:* So you're disingenuous in class.

*Professor:* What?

*Actor:* You don't tell your students what you're really up to. You're trying to convert them all. You're asking each and every one to switch sides.

*Professor:* First of all, it's a philosophy class. What do you expect? Second, my students are generally not opposed to philosophy. Most of them don't know what it is. So I'm not asking them to switch sides.

*Actor:* You're asking them to commit.

*Professor:* True. What's wrong with that?

*Director:* Maybe Actor doesn't like it because you haven't asked him to commit.

*Professor:* If you ask me, he's already committed by virtue of having this talk. Can you turn away from philosophy, Actor? I think you'll find you can't.

*Actor:* Why not?

*Professor:* Because now nothing else can satisfy.

## 58

*Actor:* Not even a system of ideas?

*Professor:* What, an ideology? Why would that satisfy you?

*Actor:* Because it would relieve me of the burden to think.

*Director:* Oh, he's just teasing, Professor.

*Actor:* But really, don't ideologies do just that?

*Director:* For those who follow blindly, yes. But for some others they can stir up thought.

*Actor:* How?

*Director:* In every ideology I've examined, something just doesn't add up.

*Actor:* And that makes you think.

*Director:* Yes.

*Actor:* What makes me think is when everything seems fine in theory, but when you try to implement the theory in practice, something goes very wrong.

*Professor:* But people put up with the wrong because they love the theory. And that's because ideas are seductive. It takes a fair amount of experience with these things not to be seduced. Ideologies often prey on inexperienced youth.

*Actor:* Inexperienced in what? Life?

*Professor:* Life, yes. But more specifically, ideas.

*Actor:* And what sort of experience with them do you need?

*Director:* You need to know how to weigh them.

*Actor:* Are you saying anything that weighs much is true?

*Director:* No, some very heavy things are false. Sorry I wasn't more clear. You determine whether they're true or false, and then you find out how much they weigh.

*Actor:* How much an idea weighs. What does that mean?

*Director:* The impact it has on life.

*Actor:* But a false idea might have a great impact.

*Director:* That would be a weighty false idea.

*Actor:* So we get rid of the idea.

*Director:* Yes, but there's a problem. We can rid ourselves of the idea—but it may still affect others.

*Actor:* How can we help?

*Director:* Sometimes all we can do is add truth to the opposite scale.

*Actor:* We want truth to outweigh the false.

*Director:* Yes.

*Professor:* If a false idea is very heavy we have to be careful how much truth we add.

*Actor:* Why?

*Professor:* There's a danger we might break the scale.

*Actor:* What does that mean? The person snaps?

*Professor:* Yes.

*Actor:* Well, that's no good. So we add a little truth. What then?

*Professor:* We try to take some of the false away.

*Actor:* And when we do?

*Professor:* We add a little more truth.

*Actor:* But what if the person has only one great big false idea? There is no 'little of the false' to take away. What then?

*Professor:* Before I say what must be done, I want to note that this is very rare.

*Actor:* Rare? Why?

*Professor:* Because false ideas tend to breed other false notions.

*Actor:* But let's suppose you find just one. What must be done?

*Professor:* You burden the opposite scale with truth... and then take cover.

## 59

*Actor:* By 'burden', what do you mean?

*Professor:* To boldly speak truth.

*Actor:* But even if you do, they won't believe you.

*Professor:* Director? You have experience with this.

*Director:* You have to establish a reputation for truth with the person in question.

*Actor:* You do this first, before speaking boldly?

*Director:* That's right.

*Actor:* So what is it? Your reputation against the deeply held false idea?

*Director:* That's it.

*Actor:* But that's not much.

*Director:* Thanks.

*Actor:* Oh, you know what I mean.

*Professor:* I know what Director means. You offer living proof against the falseness of an idea.

*Actor:* Isn't it arrogant to think you're the truth? And, what, the one under the spell of the false idea has to become the truth, too?

*Professor:* Not 'the' truth. Our truth. We each must find our own truth, our own idea.

*Actor:* What if we find an idea that others have already found? What if many others have already found it?

*Director:* Do you have a problem with that?

*Actor:* I want to be an individual.

*Professor:* No collective ideas for you?

*Actor:* Would you choose a collective idea?

*Professor:* Why does it matter what I think? Would you?

*Actor:* I've never been much of a team sports player.

*Director:* Movies aren't made by teams?

*Actor:* You know what I mean.

*Director:* You're the alpha male in the team.

*Actor:* I'm not saying that.

*Professor:* Movies are made by a collective.

*Actor:* What are you talking about? Collectives never truly exist in real life. At least they never get anything done.

*Director:* What's the closest they come?

*Actor:* Certain families are like collectives. But even they aren't fully functioning.

*Professor:* You mean they're not pure.

*Actor:* Yes.

*Director:* Why not? The alphas again?

*Actor:* People tend to organize around powerful individuals, even within all but perfect collectivist groups.

*Professor:* What about the other side, those who strive to live as individuals? Can they live the pure idea?

*Actor:* It's rare for an individual to stand perfectly on their own.

*Director:* But it's possible?

*Actor:* It's possible.

*Professor:* I'd say it's possible for the other side, too, for people to be perfectly subordinated to a group.

*Director:* I agree with that.

*Actor:* But who defines the group? Who says what it is?

*Professor:* The group itself says what it is.

*Actor:* And what will a group say it is?

*Professor:* What else but what it is?

*Actor:* But what is it?

*Professor:* Its organizing idea. Without an idea, there can be no group.

*Actor:* Can there be more than one idea?

*Professor:* There can. But they tend to create fault lines within the whole.

*Actor:* So it's best for the group to be single minded with just one idea?

*Professor:* One dominant idea, yes.

*Actor:* Is it best for an individual to have just one idea?

*Professor:* No, it's not best.

*Actor:* Why not?

*Professor:* Because then you put on blinders.

*Actor:* And the group doesn't? Tell us, Director. Are philosophers blinded?

*Director:* I hope not. Philosophers try to see all ideas for what they are, including their own.

*Actor:* Philosophy is comprehensive?

*Director:* As comprehensive as can be.


## 60

*Actor:* Can philosophy exist in a collective?

*Director:* Well, let me ask you this. Can philosophers exist as individuals?

*Actor:* Of course.

*Director:* Then I see no reason why they couldn't exist in a collective.

*Actor:* You don't really mean it.

*Director:* But I do.

*Actor:* But you can't be what you are in a collective. To be an individual is to be exactly what you are—philosophers included.

*Professor:* I think you can be what you are in a collective.

*Actor:* How?

*Professor:* What you are is a member of the collective. Be that member fully, and you are what you are.

*Actor:* But it's better to be an individual.

*Professor:* I'm not so sure.

*Actor:* Why not?

*Professor:* I've never been a member of a collective. So how can I compare?

*Actor:* Oh, that's ridiculous.

*Director:* Have you been a member of a collective, Actor?

*Actor:* Of course not.

*Director:* What if you think you haven't but you have?

*Actor:* How would that be possible?

*Director:* You might have been in an individualist collective.

*Actor:* Very funny.

*Director:* No, but seriously. Can't a group define itself with the individualist idea?

*Actor:* I suppose.

*Director:* Is it any less a group for it?

*Actor:* It might be the exception.

### 61

*Professor:* As the exception, the members would have to find ideas of their own. And that's the problem. That's why people join groups. It's hard to have your own ideas.

*Director:* What happens if you have no group idea and lack your own?

*Professor:* You're in a bad way. No one can exist without ideas.

*Actor:* What about someone who lives in complete isolation on an island somewhere?

*Professor:* No, those in isolation tend to have dialogues with themselves.

*Actor:* And?

*Professor:* They have to have an idea of themselves to talk to.

*Actor:* What if that idea changes?

*Professor:* A changing idea is still an idea.

*Actor:* That's an interesting concept. Can we live with only fluid ideas? Or do we need something solid?

*Professor:* I don't know. I keep switching between the two.

*Actor:* Director?

*Director:* I think it has to do with how we think of our core.

*Actor:* Our core being?

*Director:* Yes. Different philosophies and religions have different answers here.

*Actor:* How do you find what's in your core being?

*Director:* You get very quiet and listen to yourself.

*Professor:* Or you engage in dialogue with one and all until it becomes very clear.

*Actor:* And do you only find one idea when you get to the core?

*Professor:* There are usually three. A tripod on which to stand.

*Actor:* But we only need one?

*Professor:* One is all it takes.

*Actor:* If we have more than one in the core, how do we know which idea is sufficient?

*Professor:* I don't have an easy answer here. You just have to experiment and go by feel.

*Actor:* Go by feel as we tinker with our core? From the philosophy professor?

*Professor:* Well, you also need to stay calm.

*Director:* What's the best way?

*Professor:* The way to calm differs from person to person. It's a very particular thing.

*Director:* But what's the idea?

*Professor:* One person's idea of calm might be skiing down a ferocious slope. Their mind is focused and free. Another's idea might be reading a beautiful book. Again, their mind is focused and free.

*Actor:* Do you have to be focused for calm? And is it the focus that frees?

*Professor:* You tell us. Aren't you focused and free when you act?

*Actor:* I am. But is there another way?

*Director:* Let's look at it this way. What allows you to focus?

*Actor:* Calm.

*Director:* And what allows you to be free?

*Actor:* The focus that comes of calm?

*Director:* You're not sure?

*Actor:* No, I'm not.

*Director:* Then let's just say that calm, focus, and freedom are somehow of a piece.

*Actor:* They are of a piece.

*Director:* What allows us to achieve these three things?

*Actor:* That's the question.

*Professor:* And the answer is knowledge.

*Director:* Ah, what a surprise! I didn't think we'd come to the answer right away.

*Actor:* Is that the answer?

*Director:* I think it might be.

*Actor:* What's the idea of knowledge?

*Professor:* It's the opposite of ignorance and belief.

*Director:* An idea with two opposites.

*Professor:* Yes, it's in the middle. Consider the idea of 'just right'. When it comes to temperature, the opposite of just right is too hot or too cold.

*Actor:* Yes, but too hot or too cold are bad. Ignorance might be bad, but is belief?

*Professor:* When it comes to something that can be known? Yes.

*Actor:* Why?

*Professor:* Because knowledge is the target and we've missed the mark.

*Director:* Why is knowledge the target?

*Professor:* I think you're just asking to see what I say.

*Director:* What better reason to ask?

*Professor:* Knowledge is the target because with certain knowledge we can rest easy.

*Director:* And resting easy means calm, which allows us to focus?

*Professor:* Of course. And that's what makes us free.

## 62

*Actor:* Freedom derives from resting easy? I don't believe it.

*Director:* What do you believe?

*Actor:* Freedom is doing what you like. And doing is the opposite of rest.

*Professor:* Unless what you like to do is laze about.

*Director:* Yes, but a part of you might do while a part of you rests.

*Actor:* What part might do?

*Director:* The body.

*Actor:* While the mind might rest?

*Director:* Yes.

*Actor:* And when the body rests the mind might be active?

*Director:* The mind thinks, yes.

*Actor:* Thinking is doing?

*Director:* As long as it's really thinking and not ruminating, yes.

*Professor:* There's nothing more exhausting than serious thought.

*Actor:* A manual laborer might differ with you.

*Professor:* Not if they've ever struggled with a serious thought. The labor of the body is a relief compared to this.

*Director:* What's a serious thought, Professor?

*Professor:* It has to do with belief.

*Director:* You question the belief?

*Professor:* Yes. And this is the crisis.

*Actor:* What crisis?

*Professor:* You have to decide if it's true or not.

*Director:* And if it's not?

*Professor:* You set it aside.

*Director:* Tell us. Is every belief a belief in an idea?

*Professor:* What else do we believe in but ideas?

*Actor:* So if we have no ideas we can have no beliefs?

*Professor:* Yes.

*Actor:* Didn't we say everyone needs an idea? So that means everyone needs a belief?

*Professor:* Everyone needs a belief. The best belief they can have.

*Actor:* And what's the best belief?

*Professor:* The belief that has yet to be proven wrong.

*Actor:* What is that belief?

*Professor:* The belief in philosophy.

*Actor:* But the belief that philosophy does what?

*Professor:* Provides freedom, focus, and calm.

*Actor:* I don't believe it.

*Professor:* Why not?

*Actor:* Because philosophy overturns false ideas. And when you overturn an idea, it's anything but calm.

*Professor:* Yes, but surely the overturning provides freedom.

*Actor:* I'll grant you that. But what about focus?

*Director:* Hold on. You're awfully quick to grant. When a big enough idea overturns, what is there?

*Actor:* Chaos?

*Director:* Is there freedom in chaos, or the opposite?

*Actor:* Chaos makes slaves of us all.

*Director:* Then the overturning of a great idea doesn't provide freedom.

*Professor:* Even if it's a false idea?

*Director:* Even so. Unless you really think chaos is freedom.

*Professor:* So what would you have us do? Keep the idea intact?

*Actor:* Maybe we should aim for a gradual change.

*Professor:* And what would we say? Your idea is a little bit false? And a little more? And a little bit more? Until the job is done?

*Actor:* What do you recommend?

*Professor:* There's chaos on an individual level. And then there's chaos at large. The gradual change you want comes with individuals. If there are millions of people in a society, if ten people change, is that society at risk?

*Actor:* It depends on who those people are.

*Professor:* Fair enough. But let's say they're not leaders. Chaos?

*Actor:* Perhaps there's chaos for them, but not for society as a whole.

*Professor:* And when they come out of the chaos, and help overturn the bad idea in others, is there chaos at large?

*Actor:* I see where you're going. You're talking about grass roots change.

*Professor:* Call it what you will. But when it comes to great big bad ideas, this is the only way.

### 63

*Director:* Why is it the only way?

*Professor:* Why? Because if the idea is truly big and bad, you'll be persecuted for attacking it in the open.

*Actor:* If you live in a tyranny, you mean.

*Professor:* What's this? Don't you know?

*Actor:* Know what?

*Professor:* That tyranny is the only type of rule without a ruling idea. In other words, there's no big and bad idea to attack.

*Actor:* Of course there's an idea! The idea is for the tyrant to stay in power.

*Director:* What happens when tyrants lose power?

*Actor:* Often enough? They're killed.

*Director:* Do tyrants fear death?

*Actor:* I think they fear death more than any other living soul.

*Director:* Is there an idea associated with fear of death?

*Actor:* Yes—the belief that life itself, no matter the circumstances, is good.

*Director:* Can we say that fear of death, the tyrant's fear of death, depends on this idea?

*Actor:* We can, and we'd be right.

*Director:* How can we get rid of this idea?

*Actor:* We find something more important than life at any cost.

*Director:* And tyrants can't do this on their own?

*Actor:* For whatever reason, they can't.

*Director:* And is this, at heart, why they tyrannize over others?

*Actor:* I'm not sure.

*Professor:* I am. The answer is yes—but only in the final stage of tyranny.

*Actor:* What's in the first stage of tyranny?

*Professor:* Something more important than life at any cost.

*Actor:* What?

*Professor:* A longing for the immortality of fame, more often than not.

*Director:* I don't believe it.

*Actor:* What else would it be?

*Director:* The lust to rule. And you can't rule if you're dead.

*Actor:* That sounds more likely to me, Professor.

*Professor:* What's the idea behind lust to rule?

*Actor:* I'm not sure there is one. It's just a feeling.

*Professor:* You don't think ideas drive feelings?

*Director:* We can just as well say feelings drive ideas. You feel a longing to rule, so you come up with the idea that rule is good. But what do you think, Actor? How is it in your work?

*Actor:* In my work?

*Director:* Yes, what comes first, the feeling or the idea?

*Actor:* Most actors would say the idea comes first. You know from the script how your character feels. That's the idea. And that's where you start.

*Director:* But what do you say?

*Actor:* I say the feeling comes first.

*Professor:* How can you arrive at the feeling without the script?

*Actor:* Oh, I read the script. But I use my negative method.

*Professor:* Say more.

*Actor:* I don't pay attention to anything, to any idea, that says what my character feels. Instead, I work to eliminate everything my character doesn't feel. And then I'm left with the feelings.

*Professor:* The feelings? I don't understand.

*Actor:* The script might say there's only one feeling. But in my negative work I might not be able to rule out several feelings. If I can't rule them out, I rule them in. And then I have my idea.

*Director:* Well, you're the expert here. So how is it with lust to rule? Is the feeling first?

*Actor:* If it is, I know what comes next.

*Director:* What?

*Actor:* A lie.

*Professor:* Why a lie?

*Actor:* Because lust to rule is never something you can admit. But eventually the need for the lie goes away.

*Professor:* When?

*Actor:* Later, when the tyrant grows tired.

*Director:* And when you tire of lust to rule, you get the idea that life itself, no matter the quality, is good?

*Professor:* But why does that idea follow from lust to rule?

*Actor:* Because tyrants don't actually live. Not in any meaningful sense. And when they grow old and tired they want nothing more—than life.

### 64

*Director:* Tell us why they don't actually live.

*Actor:* Because tyrannical rule is all consuming.

*Director:* And if all consuming, then no room for ideas?

*Actor:* None.

*Director:* To be sure, are we saying without ideas there is no life?

*Actor:* We are.

*Director:* But I'm a little confused. Can't an idea be all consuming?

*Actor:* Of course it can. But the all consuming that comes from no idea, that's what's bad.

*Director:* Ideas are good; no idea is bad.

*Actor:* Well, there are bad ideas.

*Director:* So good ideas are good; bad ideas and no idea are bad.

*Actor:* Yes.

*Director:* And tyrants go from no idea to a bad idea.

*Actor:* They do. And that's all I think we can say for them.

*Professor:* We've found the essence of tyranny.

*Director:* We've found something about tyranny. There might be more.

*Actor:* But we three are concerned with ideas. And, as far as they go, I think we've summed things up well.

*Director:* Okay. What's next?

*Actor:* Are there any other things that can drive us without an idea?

*Professor:* I'm sure there are. To name just one, the attraction of love. But let's move on.

*Actor:* To what?

*Director:* Hold on. When speaking of love we spoke of false attractions. You're attracted until the other opens their mouth. We said this was because of our idea of love.

*Professor:* Is that what we said?

*Director:* We said something close enough. So if love has an idea, it's not one of the things that can drive us, like lust for rule, without an idea.

*Professor:* But lust for rule has its idea. An idea of what rule will be like. But when that idea proves bad, it's much harder to disengage from tyrannical rule than it is from love. And so the tyrant becomes disenchanted, more or less gradually, until mere life is all that's left.

*Actor:* Now I think we've really summed it up.

*Director:* The tyrant shifts from one bad idea to another. But can we help?

*Actor:* Help a tyrant? How?

*Director:* We teach them that mere life isn't enough. There must be something more.

*Actor:* What more can there be for them? They've burned all their bridges in life.

*Professor:* Maybe they build bridges to people who don't know them, people outside the nation or state.

*Actor:* A fresh new start?

*Professor:* Yes.

*Actor:* And what do they do with this start?

*Professor:* They do Director's 'something more'.

*Actor:* So what's the something more? Can it be philosophy?

*Director:* Before we get ahead of ourselves, what are we talking about? A vacation for the tyrant, or letting rule go and moving incognito to another land?

*Actor:* The kind of vacation we're talking about is impossible. Tyrants can't let go of their rule for however short a time. As for anything incognito, good luck with that.

*Director:* So there's no hope for the tyrant?

*Actor:* None.

### 65

*Director:* What about others?

*Actor:* What about them?

*Director:* When they're long on the political stage, is the idea mere life for them?

*Actor:* No, some of them are living life to the full.

*Director:* So what's the difference? Why is the tyrant not living life but the others are?

*Actor:* The tyrant started with a lust to rule. The others started with a simple desire.

*Professor:* I don't believe it. Plenty of the others started out with lust to rule.

*Actor:* Then what's the difference?

*Professor:* The tyrant brooked no hindrances to the object. The others more or less followed the rules.

*Actor:* So following the rules allows you to live life to the full?

*Director:* Do you want him to say the opposite is true?

*Actor:* I think it's a problem.

*Professor:* Why?

*Actor:* Because life's 'rules' can hinder life.

*Director:* Then what's the answer? To make your own rules?

*Professor:* Make them wrong and you'll hinder your life even more.

*Actor:* So make them right.

*Director:* How do we do that?

*Actor:* We test each rule for its effect on life.

*Professor:* And if a rule's effect is bad?

*Actor:* Then the answer is clear.

*Director:* And is it clear when a rule has a good effect?

*Actor:* Of course.

*Director:* Name such a rule.

*Actor:* Never do something that feels wrong.

*Professor:* But what if you have a bad idea that makes something feel wrong though it's right?

*Director:* Can you give an example?

*Professor:* Speaking your mind to a friend.

*Director:* What's the bad idea?

*Professor:* That you should never rock the boat.

*Director:* Rocking the boat feels wrong because of your idea—but it's right?

*Professor:* Sometimes it's right. Sometimes it's the only way to make a needed change.

*Director:* Change often feels wrong, doesn't it?

*Professor:* It does.

*Director:* But change is sometimes right. How do we know when it's right?

*Professor:* The situation improves.

*Director:* So the way to improvement takes us against our feelings at times. Then how do we know to follow it?

*Professor:* We reason our way through.

*Director:* Against our feelings.

*Professor:* Yes.

*Actor:* No. We reason our way to our true feelings. We go against the false.

*Director:* What's a false feeling?

*Actor:* One created by a bad idea.

*Director:* And a true feeling? One created by a good idea?

*Actor:* Origins don't matter when things feel good.

*Professor:* Do you really believe that?

*Actor:* Don't you?

### 66

*Professor:* How can you feel good if you know the origin of your feeling is bad? Doesn't conscience get in the way?

*Actor:* Not all of us have a conscience, Professor.

*Director:* What's the idea of conscience?

*Actor:* That you feel bad for doing wrong.

*Director:* Can we feel good if we don't have a conscience?

*Professor:* I don't think we can.

*Actor:* Honestly? Neither do I.

*Director:* Hmm. Now I wonder.

*Actor:* What are you wondering?

*Director:* Can't the one with no conscience feel good lying in the sun?

*Actor:* Yes, but that's not the point.

*Director:* How about feeling good enjoying a wonderful meal?

*Professor:* You're talking about pleasures of the body.

*Director:* Yes. Don't they make us feel good?

*Actor:* Sure, but not morally good.

*Director:* And conscience has to do with the moral.

*Actor:* Of course.

*Director:* And for those of us with a conscience, the moral makes us feel more-than-bodily good.

*Actor:* That's right.

*Director:* And the immoral makes us feel more-than-bodily bad.

*Actor:* Yes. And the more-than-bodily is much more intense than the bodily alone.

*Director:* Is the more-than-bodily outside the body?

*Actor:* I wouldn't say that.

*Director:* So it's in the body?

*Actor:* It's in the mind, or heart, or soul.

*Director:* All of which are in the body.

*Actor:* Well, yes.

*Director:* You don't sound convinced.

*Actor:* We like to think we're something more than flesh, blood, organs, and bones.

*Director:* This 'something more' defies our description?

*Actor:* We describe it as the human.

*Director:* And humans have consciences.

*Actor:* We forfeit our humanity without a conscience.

*Director:* We've been talking about the idea of conscience. What about the idea of humanity? Is it as simple as this? Humanity is the conscience.

*Actor:* No, it's not as simple as that.

*Director:* Humanity is the conscience and something more?

*Actor:* Yes.

*Director:* What more?

*Actor:* It's.... It's.... I don't know.

*Director:* Professor? Do you know what humanity is?

*Professor:* Humanity has always been an idea.

*Actor:* But what idea?

*Professor:* It varies.

*Director:* Is there anything in common among the variations?

*Professor:* They all seem to involve striving toward something beyond ourselves.

*Director:* We're inhuman if we don't strive?

*Actor:* That's ridiculous. Plenty of people don't strive, they just live—and they're as human as the rest.

*Director:* What are some things people strive toward?

*Actor:* Excellence, justice, the good.

*Director:* What kind of human doesn't strive toward one of these things?

*Actor:* An unhappy human.

*Director:* We have to strive toward something beyond in order to be happy?

*Actor:* Yes, I think we do.

*Director:* What do you strive toward, Actor?

*Actor:* Excellence in my craft.

*Director:* And you achieve it. Does that make you happy?

*Actor:* It does.

*Director:* But I'm surprised you gave up so easily.

*Actor:* What do you mean?

*Director:* You seemed poised to make the case that we don't need to strive. You said we can just live.

*Actor:* In our society that can be hard.

*Director:* Why?

*Actor:* If you're not striving, you sink to the bottom.

*Director:* And there's no happiness at the bottom?

*Actor:* None.

*Director:* There's only happiness at the top?

*Actor:* No, I'm not saying that.

*Director:* You can strive and fail and be happy?

*Actor:* Of course you can.

*Director:* How?

*Actor:* 'It's the journey and not the destination.'

*Professor:* Yes, Actor, I've heard that many times. But sometimes the destination gets us off a rather rocky road.

### 67

*Actor:* And sometimes when we get off that road we find ourselves in hell.

*Professor:* And that's very sad, because no one sets out for hell.

*Director:* Oh, I don't know. Some brave explorer might.

*Actor:* Be serious, Director. By definition, hell is someplace you don't want to be.

*Director:* Then we should ask ourselves how people get there.

*Actor:* They make mistakes.

*Director:* What kind of mistakes? Navigational mistakes?

*Actor:* Sure.

*Director:* So they need a compass and a map. Where do they get the compass?

*Actor:* Each of us is born with one.

*Director:* And where do we get the map?

*Actor:* That's the problem.

*Director:* How so?

*Actor:* A map is always someone else's view.

*Director:* And we need our own view to get to where we're going?

*Actor:* Yes.

*Director:* So we do without a map?

*Actor:* I'm afraid we have to.

*Director:* Then what use is a compass? Why does it matter if we know we're heading north if we have no map to follow? Maybe we need to go west? Or east? Who knows?

*Professor:* The compass is of no use.

*Director:* So we face the world with only our wits?

*Professor:* And go wherever we must. That's liberating, you know.

*Director:* So how do we not wind up in hell?

*Actor:* We make good decisions.

*Director:* And the sum of good decisions can't be bad.

*Actor:* That's absolutely true.

*Professor:* Haven't you heard that the road to hell is paved with good decisions?

*Actor:* Good intentions, Professor. Good intentions.

*Professor:* Yes, but good intentions made real still might lead to hell.

*Actor:* You're missing the point of the saying.

*Director:* The saying is optimistic—good intentions made real never lead to hell.

*Actor:* Do you doubt that's true?

*Director:* I'm inclined to think good actions can't lead to hell. But how do we know what's good?

*Professor:* It's easy in theory. But in practice? That's the question. I don't think we know until we try.

*Actor:* We can leverage the experience of those who've gone before.

*Professor:* Weren't you the one who said maps are problematic? What else is someone's experience but a map? A map of a different set of circumstances.

*Director:* And good and bad are based on circumstance?

*Professor:* In large part? Yes.

*Actor:* Then we rely on our own experience.

*Director:* I think that's the key. And if we want to go somewhere wholly new?

*Actor:* Just keep on walking in a straight line. Eventually that always takes you someplace new. But we need to be careful.

*Director:* Careful? While walking in a straight line?

*Actor:* We can't make leaps. We should only take steps.

*Director:* What's wrong with making leaps?

*Actor:* You really don't know where you'll land. With a step you more or less know.

*Director:* We need to know where we're going?

*Actor:* Yes.

*Director:* And we can only know what's before us.

*Actor:* And even then....

*Director:* Yes, even then we don't know. We don't know until we're there. So why is a leap so bad?

*Actor:* With a step the odds are better that we'll know.

*Director:* So we're playing the odds. A gamble of sorts.

*Actor:* And you know the saying—bet it all and sleep in the streets.

*Director:* So we make little bets, step by step.

*Professor:* Do you think there's something pathetic in that?

*Director:* Only to someone... with grand ideas.

### 68

*Actor:* Shouldn't we all have grand ideas? Shouldn't we dream?

*Professor:* Dream, sure. But we shouldn't walk in our sleep.

*Director:* It's philosophy's job to wake somnambulists up.

*Actor:* They say you shouldn't do that, that it's dangerous for the sleeper.

*Professor:* The real danger is to the waker. The sleeper might lash out at you.

*Actor:* Why would they do that?

*Professor:* Because you've taken their precious idea away.

*Director:* You haven't taken their idea away. You've suggested it's not what they think. Then they do the rest.

*Actor:* What's the rest?

*Director:* Retracing their steps, to see what they've done.

*Actor:* And then?

*Director:* Making things right.

*Actor:* What if the things done during sleep were right?

*Director:* Then they were done by accident.

*Actor:* Or by habit ingrained while they were awake.

*Director:* That may be. So do we only awaken those with bad habits?

*Actor:* I'd let those with good habits be.

*Director:* Professor?

*Professor:* Sometimes we're only brave enough to make a leap while we dream.

*Director:* A leap? What kind of leap?

*Professor:* From one idea to another.

*Director:* Then we need spotters who are ready to catch us if we fall.

*Actor:* That assumes they know where we're leaping from and where we're leaping to.

*Director:* And isn't it good for them to know?

*Actor:* How so? Aside from catching, whatever that means.

*Director:* You're basically asking why we should share our ideas?

*Actor:* Yes. Why?

*Director:* Because when we don't, they fester.

*Actor:* They become infected?

*Director:* Don't act surprised. If we keep them in the darkest isolation, what do you think happens? They need the light of day.

*Actor:* Daylight sanitizes things?

*Director:* Of course. The light of day with friends.

*Professor:* To be sure—there should be no isolated ideas?

*Director:* None. Get them all into the light.

*Actor:* In order to disinfect?

*Director:* In order to find the truth.

### 69

*Actor:* Festering ideas are false?

*Director:* We can't know if they're true or false until we bring them to the light.

*Actor:* And if they're false?

*Director:* We have to dispose of them.

*Actor:* And when they're true?

*Director:* Sharing them makes them stronger.

*Actor:* How?

*Director:* Friends can reinforce truth.

*Actor:* Yes, but how?

*Professor:* I'll tell you how. When a friend confirms what you think, you know you're on the right path.

*Actor:* Can't you both be wrong?

*Professor:* Sure, but it's less likely.

*Actor:* And we only care about the likely truth?

*Professor:* We care about more than that.

*Actor:* How can we get at this more-than-that?

*Professor:* We put our friends to the test.

*Actor:* And they put us to the test?

*Professor:* Everyone puts everyone to the test. How's that?

*Actor:* I think it's pretty good. We're more likely to do well that way.

*Director:* What if we're shy?

*Actor:* We don't want to be put to the test.

*Director:* Are shy ones in danger because of that?

*Actor:* They might have the wrong idea.

*Director:* And they'll never know?

*Actor:* Not unless they put themselves to the test.

*Director:* Put themselves? Without others?

*Actor:* Oh, they need others. But they learn from them and then go off on their own.

*Professor:* But what about the sunlight?

*Actor:* That's what they learn—how to make their own.

*Professor:* Artificial light?

*Actor:* What can I say? It's a wonder of technology.

*Director:* When they have their light, and they're about to examine themselves, what do they need?

*Professor:* Integrity.

*Actor:* They need more than that. They need courage.

*Director:* Courage to be honest with themselves?

*Actor:* Yes.

*Director:* If you need courage, that suggests there must be fear. Why would you be afraid to be honest with yourself?

*Actor:* You might have to change what you think, change your ideas. Fundamental change always frightens.

*Professor:* Yes, and there are two challenges here—inner and outer.

*Director:* Tell us about the outer.

*Professor:* It has to do with integrity. And integrity involves consistency.

*Actor:* Consistency? Why?

*Professor:* Where's your integrity if you're inconsistent in everything you do?

*Actor:* Are you saying it's better to be consistent and wrong than change—however often—and be right?

*Director:* I don't think he's saying that. Are you, Professor?

*Professor:* No. But it's hard to change. And frequent change has consequences.

*Director:* How can we minimize the negative consequences?

*Professor:* We let our new idea grow strong inside before we expose it to the world.

*Actor:* Isn't that dishonest?

*Professor:* What do you mean?

*Actor:* Suppose a time comes, while you're hatching your new idea, when you're expected to make a difficult stand on the old one. Do you hold fast to a principle you no longer believe?

*Professor:* Well, that's the problem.

*Actor:* So you release your new view to the world even though it's not ready.

*Director:* People might think you're making an opportunistic change.

*Actor:* Then we announce the change in idea before it comes to that.

70

*Director:* I have a question. We've used 'idea', and 'principle', and 'view' interchangeably. Are they really interchangeable?

*Professor:* They are, though they suggest different things.

*Director:* Can you give us an example?

*Professor:* Yes, but first we should note another word that's interchangeable with all of them.

*Director:* Oh? What word?

*Professor:* Belief. Now here's the example. I believe it's never right to lie. I stand on the principle that it's never right to lie. I hold the view that it's never right to lie. I have the idea that it's never right to lie. You see? They're all the same but they suggest slightly different things.

*Director:* Can we know all the things our words suggest?

*Actor:* All of them? Of course not.

*Director:* Why not?

*Actor:* Because suggestion is highly personal.

*Director:* What makes it highly personal?

*Actor:* Language is tied up with experience, which lives in memory. We all have different experiences. We all have different memories. So we each experience language in a different way.

*Director:* Why is language tied up with experience?

*Actor:* It just... is!

*Director:* Professor?

*Professor:* It's an open question. I can learn what the word bonobo means while never experiencing anything to do with the animal itself.

*Actor:* Yes, but you'll remember your experience of learning the word.

*Professor:* Will I? Do I remember the experience of learning the word cat? I don't. And yet I know the word perfectly well.

*Actor:* Yes, but your idea of cat will be different than mine.

*Professor:* If we put out pictures of animals and try to identify the cat, you and I will almost certainly agree.

*Actor:* But the word will have different associations with the two of us.

*Professor:* Ah, associations, yes.

*Actor:* That's where suggestions come in.

*Director:* So if you got badly scratched by a cat, you might think of scratches when I say cat, but I might not?

*Actor:* Yes.

*Director:* And this is so with all words or ideas?

*Actor:* No doubt.

*Professor:* Then we never have hold of a pure idea. It's always colored by our experiences.

*Director:* Tell us, Professor. Do common experiences make for a language?

*Professor:* There might be something to that. Haven't you heard people say, "We have our own private language here"?

*Director:* I have. And I think it's because of common experience. Actor, do you agree?

*Actor:* I do. But is that how major languages form? From common experience?

*Director:* It might be.

*Professor:* Yes, but if I learn a language on my own from an online course, I don't need common experience with native speakers.

*Actor:* You might know the words, but do you really understand the meaning?

*Director:* We might ask that of native speakers of our own language.

*Actor:* I think there are layers of meaning.

*Director:* The surface meaning and those more profound?

*Actor:* Yes. The most profound meaning is with someone you love.

*Director:* Why is that? Because you have more common experience with someone you love? What does that mean for love at first sight?

*Actor:* We might love at first sight because we recognize the marks of shared experience.

*Director:* You were both badly scratched by metaphorical cats, for instance— and it shows.

*Actor:* Yes.

*Director:* Well, there might be something to it, something profound. But can we get by with just the surface meaning?

*Actor:* We can get by, yes. But we won't share something more.

*Professor:* Who wouldn't want something more?

*Actor:* Those who just want to get by.

*Director:* But who just wants to get by?

*Actor:* You'd be surprised. There are many.

*Director:* Getting by is more important than depth of meaning?

*Actor:* For the shallow it is.

*Director:* In a conversation, how can we tell if someone is shallow?

*Actor:* Their souls aren't deepened by any long held ideas.

*Director:* And in language ideas are words.

*Actor:* Yes.

*Director:* So if they don't have any long held words, we know they're shallow.

*Professor:* True, but long held words don't necessarily make you deep. I know shallow people who have very long held words—the words money, profit, advantage.

*Director:* So it's not the length a word-idea is held.

*Actor:* I do think it's the length, but I think it has to be a certain kind of word.

*Director:* A deep word?

*Actor:* Yes, like love.

*Professor:* But there are different kinds of love.

*Actor:* Of course. But the deepest of love, when held a long while, deepens the soul.

*Director:* I think you're on to something there. But what other word-ideas can deepen the soul like this?

*Actor:* Patriotism, for example.

*Professor:* But that's just another kind of love. Can you give us another?

*Actor:* Self-worth.

*Professor:* Which is to say self-love. Can't you think of a deepening word that doesn't involve love?

*Actor:* I... can't.

## 71

*Professor:* Director?

*Director:* I'm at a loss.

*Professor:* Well, I can't think of one either.

*Director:* But wait. What about those long in the habit of thinking complex thoughts?

*Actor:* Yes, complexity isn't typically on the surface. It goes to the depths.

*Director:* But even if it's a combination of just two words, would it make for depth?

*Actor:* I don't know. We have the money and profit example. Someone could spend a lifetime combining these two words—and be none the deeper.

*Director:* The words matter.

*Actor:* Of course they do.

*Director:* What if one of the words is 'ambition' and the other is the object of that ambition?

*Actor:* No, I don't think that necessarily makes for depth. You can be very ambitious for money and profit, you know—and stay on the surface of things.

*Director:* What if the object of the ambition is high?

*Actor:* You mean like high office?

*Director:* Sure. What do you think? Would long contemplation of that make you deep?

*Actor:* You have to aim high to go deep? Maybe.

*Professor:* Maybe indeed. But not necessarily. I think the depth here again comes from love. Self-love.

*Director:* But the one with money and profit in mind can have self-love. Does that make them deep?

*Professor:* They have to have something else in mind for depth.

*Actor:* Of course they do—because money and profit alone aren't good.

*Director:* Is self-love, alone, good?

*Actor:* You should tell me.

*Director:* Why?

*Actor:* Because self-love is what a philosopher has.

*Director:* Can you say more?

*Actor:* A philosopher's drive to know comes from self-love—because the philosopher knows the more that's known the better the self.

*Director:* So the best souls belong to those who know many facts?

*Actor:* You can know many facts and still not know the important things.

*Director:* Things like love?

*Actor:* Yes.

*Director:* Well, I'm all in favor of philosophers coming to know love. I'm all in favor of everyone coming to know love.

*Professor:* The more they know of it the better they'll be. But what does it mean to know love?

*Actor:* To experience love.

*Professor:* And all of us can experience love? Or are some not fit?

*Actor:* Well, it depends.

*Professor:* On what?

*Actor:* What belief about love you hold.

*Professor:* What are the beliefs you can have?

*Actor:* One says all of us can experience love; another says only some of us can.

*Professor:* But those aren't the only beliefs.

*Actor:* What else is there?

*Professor:* Belief in the power of love.

*Actor:* I believe in love's power but not its universality.

*Director:* Who can't experience the power of love?

*Actor:* Those who are rotten beyond repair.

*Director:* Are you smuggling in an idea?

*Actor:* What idea?

*Director:* That everyone is born open to the power of love, but as we grow some of us rot.

*Actor:* Yes, I like that idea. Let's smuggle it in.

*Director:* Okay. But why do some of us rot?

*Actor:* Because we make bad choices.

*Director:* So there's a moral factor here?

*Actor:* If you think choices are moral, yes.

*Director:* You don't think the idea of choices is necessarily moral?

*Actor:* First, why is 'choices' an idea?

*Director:* Because there's another idea that says we make no real choices in life. We're determined by circumstances in whatever we do.

*Actor:* No, that's nonsense. We all have some choice.

*Director:* Professor, did you hear him hedge?

*Professor:* 'Some choice', yes. We don't always have much choice. But the choice we do have renders us fit for love or not. Is that the idea, Actor?

*Actor:* That's the idea.

*Director:* Is this a long held view with you?

*Actor:* From as far back as I can remember.

*Director:* Then it's high time to shine the light.

### 72

*Actor:* Where do we begin?

*Professor:* We start with what makes us fit for love.

*Director:* But we have to be clear. Are we talking about being fit to love, or fit to be loved?

*Professor:* Both. They're one and the same.

*Director:* Really? Then what makes us fit?

*Actor:* Humility.

*Director:* Humility?

*Actor:* Why, do you have a problem with that?

*Director:* I'm not sure if I do or I don't.

*Actor:* How can we help you settle your mind?

*Director:* Just tell the truth. Do you love the humble?

*Actor:* Not all of the humble, of course not.

*Director:* But those you love must be humble, not proud?

*Actor:* You can be proud and humble at once.

*Director:* Proud and humble at once? How?

*Actor:* You can be proud of who you are, but humble toward others.

*Professor:* Why would you do that? Be humble, I mean.

*Actor:* Others might be better than you at something.

*Professor:* Do you love them for this something better?

*Actor:* I do.

*Professor:* And they love you for your something better?

*Actor:* In the ideal, yes.

*Director:* What if you're both good at the same thing?

*Actor:* That makes for danger.

*Director:* Danger? Why?

*Actor:* Because you might compete.

*Professor:* An intra-love rivalry.

*Actor:* Right.

*Director:* And lovers shouldn't be rivals.

*Actor:* It puts a damper on the love.

*Professor:* Or it could make you both better.

*Actor:* Best to rely on others for that.

*Director:* Why?

*Actor:* Because you might not get better through rivalry. And if you don't, you might be bitter toward your love.

*Professor:* Tell us, Actor. Do we love those who make us better?

*Actor:* We should.

*Professor:* So we might love someone other than our beloved—if they make us better, that is.

*Actor:* Yes, but it's not the same sort of love.

*Director:* It's more shallow?

*Actor:* No, I wouldn't say that.

*Director:* What is it?

*Actor:* It's not romantic, that's what.

*Professor:* Romantic. What's the idea of the romantic?

*Actor:* That we have one exclusive love.

*Professor:* One exclusive romantic love, but many other sorts of love?

*Actor:* Exactly.

*Professor:* What makes the one exclusive?

*Actor:* You have the deepest sort of bond.

*Professor:* Does love always involve a bond?

*Actor:* Even non-romantic love? Yes, I think it does

*Professor:* What about fleeting love? I mean, you might meet someone who's a natural friend, and have love for them. But you go your separate ways.

*Actor:* Love needs to be nourished by contact for the bond to grow strong.

*Director:* The bond, maybe. But what about the love itself? Can't love be at its maximum right from the start?

*Actor:* Well, yes.

*Professor:* So it never gets better?

*Actor:* In some cases? True. But that doesn't mean it has to get worse. It evolves into something deeper.

*Professor:* But doesn't 'deeper' mean more love?

*Actor:* Evolution involves taking your love to new places.

*Director:* What, like going on trips?

*Actor:* No. Journeys together, journeys of the heart and mind.

*Professor:* Give us an example.

*Actor:* You devote yourselves to a cause.

*Director:* And that makes you closer?

*Actor:* You're already close. The point is that the cause takes you new places.

*Director:* What's good about a new place?

*Actor:* It gives you, as a person, the opportunity to grow.

### 73

*Director:* Is growth a sign of fitness for love?

*Actor:* I think that's fair to say.

*Director:* What if you grow and your love doesn't? Does that affect the love?

*Actor:* Not necessarily.

*Director:* Why not?

*Actor:* Your love might love you for having grown. And you might love your love for loving you for having grown.

*Professor:* Yes, yes. But we should say a word about growth. There's an idea out there that growth is always good.

*Actor:* Not if you're gaining too much weight.

*Professor:* Yes, but do you agree that for the most part people see growth as good?

*Actor:* I agree. Economic growth especially.

*Professor:* But also growth in love, growth in maturity, growth in understanding—and so on.

*Actor:* Yes, people are always talking about these things. But I'd collapse maturity and understanding into one.

*Professor:* That's fine. Let's speak of understanding. What does it mean to grow in understanding?

*Actor:* To understand more.

*Professor:* More what?

*Actor:* More... things.

*Professor:* So if I understand what more and more people think, is that the kind of 'more things' you have in mind?

*Actor:* Sure.

*Professor:* But won't many people think the same things?

*Actor:* That's likely.

*Professor:* So I can reduce it down to the common thoughts. Maybe that's not so many things.

*Actor:* Maybe it's not.

*Professor:* But how well do I understand these thoughts? Let's say there are ten.

*Actor:* Ten, okay.

*Professor:* Do I grow in understanding if I take two of these thoughts and spend a long time with them?

*Actor:* You should.

*Professor:* How does that process work?

*Actor:* You come to see the thoughts in many different lights, from many angles.

*Professor:* So you get a real feel for the thoughts.

*Actor:* Yes.

*Professor:* And this feel is what we call understanding.

*Actor:* It is.

*Professor:* Is there any other way to get a feel for a thing than what we've described?

*Actor:* Some people get the feel at first sight.

*Professor:* Some people are predisposed to understand?

*Actor:* They are.

*Professor:* And when they understand it at once, they understand in full?

*Actor:* Yes.

*Professor:* Are you sure? In full?

*Actor:* Yes, I'm sure.

*Professor:* Then how can they ever hope to grow in understanding?

*Actor:* You grow by learning what to do with the thing.

*Professor:* Ah. So you can understand but not know what to do.

*Actor:* Of course.

*Professor:* You don't understand the larger circumstances, the situation.

*Actor:* That's exactly what you don't understand. If you did, you'd know what to do.

*Professor:* So while understanding the thing, you can grow in your understanding of the situation.

*Actor:* Right.

*Professor:* Can you understand the situation but not the thing?

*Actor:* I don't see why not.

*Professor:* Isn't the thing part of the situation?

*Actor:* You make a fair point.

*Professor:* To understand the situation in full you need to understand everything in it. But that includes... you. Doesn't it?

*Actor:* You're part of the situation, sure.

*Professor:* So you have to understand yourself.

*Actor:* Yes.

*Professor:* And once you've understood one situation, you might go on to understand another?

*Actor:* You very well might.

*Professor:* If you go from understanding one situation to two, have you grown?

*Actor:* I'd say you have.

*Professor:* Are there only so many situations to master?

*Actor:* No, they're never ending.

*Professor:* Because they're infinite, or because they always change?

*Actor:* Practically speaking they're infinite, and they always change.

*Professor:* So we could exhaust ourselves trying to master situations.

*Actor:* I'd be happy to master one and keep an eye on it while it changes.

*Professor:* And isn't that how it is with love? You can have one love, but it's always changing.

*Actor:* Of course. So you have to master it—and keep an eye on it, too.

## 74

*Director:* It sounds funny to say you'd master love.

*Actor:* What would you have us say?

*Director:* That we accommodate love.

*Professor:* Love is the fact and we must adjust?

*Director:* Why not? After all, isn't that a good way to simplify things?

*Actor:* What do you mean?

*Director:* Do you agree our feelings are often mixed?

*Actor:* Of course. We have many of them and confuse them all the time.

*Director:* Are we in danger of confusing love?

*Actor:* No, the attraction of love is clear.

*Director:* So if we concentrate there...

*Actor:* ...we're free. Unless we have bad ideas.

*Director:* What bad ideas?

*Actor:* Those that say your attraction is bad.

*Director:* Can you give us an example?

*Actor:* You might be attracted to unconventional beauty. But you have the idea that conventional beauty is good. You think your attraction is bad and seek convention—because you're confused.

*Director:* What do you think your attraction is? Can you say more than it's bad?

*Actor:* It's something that pulls you down from the heights of conventional success.

*Director:* So there are two ideas here. The idea of love, or attraction; and the idea of success, or ambition.

*Professor:* Ambition in love is a terrible thing. The two ideas should never mix.

*Director:* What happens when they do?

*Professor:* You're never quite happy in love.

*Director:* Are there other ideas that shouldn't mix?

*Professor:* Ambition shouldn't mix with much.

*Director:* What's something it should mix with?

*Professor:* It should mix with the idea of excellence.

*Director:* If you're excellent you deserve success?

*Professor:* Yes.

*Director:* Actor, you're excellent at what you do. You're ambitious here. And you deserve success.

*Actor:* Thank you.

*Director:* But what kind of success?

*Actor:* What do you mean?

*Director:* Conventional success?

*Actor:* Oh, I see. No, not necessarily.

*Director:* What's unconventional success?

*Actor:* Only one person recognizing your excellence for what it is.

*Professor:* And if you and that person are in love?

*Actor:* So much the better.

*Director:* Is this the kind of success you truly want? Recognition by one?

*Actor:* Honestly? No.

*Director:* So is it better if two people recognize your excellence?

*Actor:* We're getting closer, but it's still not the success I want.

*Director:* What's your idea of success? Ten people? A hundred?

*Actor:* Success for me is in the millions.

*Director:* And they, these millions, recognize your excellence for what it is?

*Actor:* Yes.

*Director:* And are you happy with that?

*Actor:* Of course.

*Director:* So you don't need love to find happiness.

*Actor:* Well, my fans love me.

*Director:* Do you love them?

*Actor:* I do.

*Professor:* So you do need love to find happiness.

*Actor:* It's true. And love should permeate all. Just like goodness.

*Director:* Are there any other ideas that should permeate all?

*Professor:* The idea of philosophy.

*Actor:* Oh, why ruin love with philosophy?

*Professor:* Ruin? Philosophy enhances love.

*Actor:* How?

*Professor:* It purifies love by making it known for what it is.

*Actor:* And what is it?

*Professor:* Haven't we been over this, my friend? The point is that philosophy separates love from the dross.

*Director:* Dross like ambition?

*Professor:* Yes. Philosophy shows that love and ambition don't mix.

### 75

*Actor:* Does philosophy show it? Or does it just state it as a fact? I'm ambitious in my career. And there's love in what I do.

*Director:* Is your ambition an ambition for love?

*Actor:* I want my fans to love me.

*Director:* And you're ambitious to grow this love to ever more fans?

*Actor:* Yes.

*Director:* What do you expect from an individual fan?

*Actor:* I want them to love my work. And that love leads to love for me.

*Director:* What if they love your work but don't love you? After all, they don't know you. Can you be happy with that?

*Actor:* You're asking me to be honest. No, they don't know me. So how can I be happy with their love? I can only be happy with their love for my work.

*Director:* Let me press you a bit. You said you love your fans. But you don't know them.

*Actor:* I love them for loving my work. And I know they love my work.

*Director:* Is it fair to say you love the love of your work?

*Actor:* What I love is love? I'm not sure that's fair. I love the one who loves.

*Director:* But only in their love. Again, you know nothing about them other than their love. They could be otherwise rotten people.

*Actor:* But doesn't loving my work imply they're good?

*Director:* A thief might love your work. Does that make her or him good?

*Actor:* The part that loves is good.

*Director:* Because your work is good.

*Actor:* Yes. And good is attracted to good.

*Professor:* But what if you play the part of a thief, and the real life thief loves you in the role? Is good still attracted to good?

*Actor:* The part of the thief that loves the truth loves my realistic portrayal of the life of a thief. I wouldn't romanticize it, if that's what you were wondering.

*Director:* I think he has a point, Professor. The truth-loving part of a soul is good. It loves portrayals of truth. The ones portraying that truth love to be loved by this good part of the soul. It all seems good to me.

*Actor:* And me.

*Professor:* Are there any ideas in conflict here?

*Actor:* None.

*Professor:* Director?

*Director:* Well, there might be one.

*Actor:* What idea?

*Director:* Distortion.

*Actor:* Distortion? What are you talking about?

*Director:* Your mention of romanticization made me wonder. What if you and the thief are wrong in your notion of reality, of truth?

*Actor:* You mean, I'm really not portraying the truth.

*Director:* Right. And the thief isn't thinking the truth. But since you think alike, incorrectly though it may be—you both love.

*Actor:* But that's not conflict. We're in harmony.

*Director:* It's a conflict with the idea of truth.

*Actor:* But we have the same idea of truth.

*Director:* But it's not the truth.

*Professor:* How many people do you think share distorted notions of truth?

*Director:* Many. They share the same distorted ideas.

*Actor:* How can an idea be distorted?

*Director:* With the idea of truth, for instance, people might settle for truth enough. Over time their idea of truth becomes distorted. It's not clearly in view.

*Professor:* Director, would you say that all ideas distort when not clearly in view?

*Director:* Yes, and this explains philosophy's habit of going over the same things again and again from different points of view. It wants to keep things clear.

*Actor:* Is philosophy the love of clear ideas?

*Director:* Philosophy is the love of making them clear.

*Actor:* Then what's the love of clear ideas?

*Professor:* I'll tell you what it is, Actor. Salvation.

## 76

*Actor:* Yes, Professor, but you can love clear ideas and not have them.

*Professor:* Then you'd better become a philosopher.

*Director:* Actor, do you believe those who engage with philosophers are philosophers if only for a time?

*Actor:* I do. So I'm a philosopher today.

*Professor:* You'll take whatever clear ideas you can and run off with them?

*Actor:* No, I'll walk. It's less conspicuous that way.

*Director:* Why not become a philosopher yourself?

*Actor:* I'd rather act than philosophize. Besides, philosophy doesn't pay the rent.

*Professor:* It pays my rent.

*Actor:* Teaching pays your rent, not philosophy.

*Director:* However that may be, what's the difference between acting and philosophy? Can't actors make ideas clear?

*Actor:* You know, they can—given the right script.

*Director:* Someone with your level of success can surely have their choice of roles.

*Actor:* True, to some extent.

*Director:* So why not choose roles that make things clear?

*Actor:* What kinds of things do you think an audience would like clear?

*Director:* Anything that's generally befogged.

*Actor:* Befogged. Funny. How about this? Ideas about who we are.

*Director:* Sure.

*Actor:* Ideas about what the government is.

*Director:* Why not? But you've covered a lot of ground.

*Professor:* Oh, he can get more particular. All he has to do is read the headline news to find dozens of specific ideas at once.

*Actor:* Don't you think everyone in the entertainment industry is already doing just that?

*Professor:* Then why haven't they dispelled the fog?

*Actor:* Maybe we're all incompetent.

*Professor:* No, that seems unlikely to me. I rather think there are many highly competent people at work.

*Actor:* Then why the fog?

*Professor:* Because they know how to play to the fog, without reducing it one bit.

*Actor:* You're saying the audience likes the fog?

*Professor:* Some do. And some take the fog because that's all they think they can get. You should play to the latter.

*Actor:* Who do you think I play to now?

*Professor:* Do you really want me to say?

*Actor:* You're saying I deal in fog?

*Professor:* I'm trying to recall something you've done that makes things clear.

*Director:* I can think of something. I saw an interview with you once. You said you loved every role you'd ever had, and that was the secret to your success.

*Actor:* What was I making clear?

*Director:* The ideas of love and success.

*Actor:* Can you say more?

*Director:* To love a role. What does that mean?

*Actor:* To embrace what you're given and make it your own.

*Director:* Because what you make your own you love.

*Actor:* Yes.

*Director:* That's clear. As for success? Let me have a go at what you meant. People love it when they get the sense you love your role.

*Actor:* Of course. But it's not enough to love. A bad actor can love a role. You have to make it your own, as we've said.

*Director:* And people want to see your own.

*Actor:* Yes, they do.

*Director:* Bad actors can't make a role their own?

*Actor:* No, they can't. So what have I made clear?

*Director:* What people want and what you've got. When the two combine, there's success. But that's not really a secret, is it?

*Actor:* No, it's no secret.

*Director:* So why did you say it was?

*Actor:* I don't know. It's just a saying, a turn of phrase.

*Professor:* Philosophy is opposed to empty turns of phrase.

*Actor:* So what should I have said?

*Professor:* 'That's the reason for my success.'

*Actor:* Next time that's what I'll say.

*Director:* Good. But here's the problem. What if you make a befogged character your own?

*Actor:* I've done that, you know.

*Director:* Have you? How did it go over?

*Actor:* Very well. I won an award.

*Director:* Why do you think you did?

*Actor:* Because it's hard to portray the befogged.

*Director:* Is it? You would know. But why else do you think you won the award?

*Actor:* What do you mean?

*Professor:* I know what he means. You won because people love their own.

*Director:* So the befogged love the befogged. And while they might respect your ability to portray the un-befogged, the clear—they won't really like it.

*Actor:* You two want me to portray only the clear?

*Professor:* No, depict the fog—but make it clear it's bad.

### 77

*Actor:* Are most people befogged?

*Professor:* I can only tell you about my students and me. We all have some fog. But we aim to clear it up.

*Actor:* Your classroom is a rarified space. If even you have some fog, what will my audience have?

*Professor:* I honestly don't know. Maybe people come to philosophy class because they know they're more befogged than most.

*Director:* Most people are befogged at some time in their life.

*Actor:* So you're asking me to lose my audience. Who wants to see a show where who they are, or were, is bashed?

*Director:* Who said anything about bashing? You need to be subtle, my friend.

*Actor:* Subtly show them that being befogged is bad?

*Director:* Yes.

*Actor:* How?

*Director:* By showing how good it is to be clear. The contrast is all. You can do this with a minor character. The character can show it's good to be clear.

*Actor:* That's good. Minor characters almost never lose an audience. The audience can write them off as... minor.

*Professor:* People love the major and neglect the minor.

*Director:* I used to focus so much on the minor that I was at a loss to describe the major.

*Actor:* You must have seemed like a fool.

*Director:* Yes. But I learned.

*Actor:* Now you pay attention to both?

*Director:* I do. And I love to see how the minor influence the major. In bad shows the minor are swept aside with no impact on the plot.

*Actor:* Then why include them?

*Director:* Exactly. Good shows have the minor make their mark.

*Actor:* Are the minor clear when it comes to ideas?

*Director:* It can go either way. But it should be the opposite of the major characters.

*Actor:* So if the major are clear, the minor should be befogged? And if the major are befogged, the minor should be clear?

*Director:* That's how it seems to me. It's good dramatic tension that way.

*Professor:* And if they're the same? No tension?

*Director:* There is no tension between the clear. Not inherent tension, at least. But I think there's tension between the befogged.

*Actor:* Why?

*Professor:* Because there's only one way to be right, and there are a million ways to be wrong.

*Actor:* I don't know about that, Professor.

*Director:* You think there's only one way to be wrong?

*Actor:* No, I doubt whether there's only one way to be right.

*Professor:* Two plus two is four. That's the one right way. Or we could say A is A, if you prefer logic. We could be wrong in each of these in a million ways. But only these two are right.

*Actor:* But A can be B.

*Professor:* B is different than A. As is C, D, E, and so on. It's wrong to say A is anything other than A. It's the law of identity.

*Actor:* I don't know about this law, or whatever else you're trying to say.

*Director*: Is that because you're not A?

*Actor*: What do you mean?

*Director*: You play character A. But you're not that character. You're not A.

*Actor*: Well, no one is ever exactly what the script says. And that's a good thing. You add your touch. You fill in the blanks.

*Professor*: What if the blanks were meant to be blanks?

*Actor*: The audience generally doesn't like blanks.

*Director*: They want you to spell it all out?

*Actor*: Even in mysteries, they want it spelled out in the end.

*Professor*: You don't want to leave your audience unsatisfied.

*Actor*: Right. They want to be satisfied. That's my goal.

*Director*: And if they're satisfied with fog?

*Actor*: In that case, you don't want me to act for them?

*Director*: No, I don't.

*Actor*: So I'll only satisfy those who want clear ideas?

*Director*: Yes, by making the clear ideas triumph. And you'll be quite the actor in this.

*Actor*: You don't think it's been done before?

*Director*: It probably has. But it's not common.

*Actor*: But, really, what are we talking about? So many stories end with the triumph of love. Isn't that a clear idea?

*Director*: It can be. How is it with you?

*Actor*: With me? I don't know. Love is love.

*Professor*: Yes, but clear love makes you better than you were.

*Actor*: What is 'better'?

*Professor*: Happier.

*Actor*: So you'd teach people to rely on love for happiness?

*Professor*: No, not only that.

*Actor*: Why not?

*Professor*: Because that's a recipe for disaster.

*Actor*: How so?

*Professor*: Happy love happens when two happy people combine.

*Actor:* You have to be happy on your own when you find love?

*Professor:* And your lover must be happy, too.

*Actor:* Director, what do you think about this?

*Director:* I want to know if love is such a fragile thing that it takes so much happiness to make it succeed.

*Professor:* Fragile? It might not be fragile. But it's no panacea, as it's often portrayed. And that's the fog. That love cures all.

*Director:* Actor, have you played in roles where love cures all?

*Actor:* Of course I have. It's the most common role of all.

*Director:* Do you think it's true? Does love cure all?

*Actor:* It can, for a while. But love like that never lasts.

*Professor:* And if it doesn't have to cure all? If there's happiness supporting the love?

*Actor:* Then the love lasts. Because two strong ones make a better... two.

## 78

*Professor:* But you say 'strong' not 'happy'.

*Actor:* You have to be strong to be happy.

*Professor:* Why?

*Actor:* Because happiness requires a constant fight.

*Professor:* But you can be strong and lose the battle.

*Actor:* Yes, of course.

*Professor:* What makes you win?

*Actor:* You have to have the right ideas.

*Professor:* Ideas about what?

*Actor:* The weaknesses of your foes.

*Professor:* I thought you were talking about an inner fight.

*Actor:* Every outer fight has an inner component; but every inner fight has an outer one, too.

*Director:* The right ideas make you fight well?

*Actor:* Yes, and if you're strong—you'll conquer.

*Director:* Can you give an example of this?

*Actor:* Say your opponent likes to brag. You need to know what it means to brag.

*Director:* That's not hard.

*Actor:* No, but you need to know this well, well enough to exploit.

*Director:* How well is well enough to exploit?

*Actor:* Profoundly well.

*Professor:* So how do you exploit a brag?

*Actor:* You call them on it. You challenge them to live up to their boast.

*Professor:* And when they can't, you've won?

*Actor:* No. They can often live up to their brag.

*Professor:* Then I don't understand.

*Actor:* When they live up to it, they feel triumphant. And that's when you strike.

*Professor:* Strike what?

*Actor:* What they haven't got, the things they never mention.

*Director:* Things you yourself have.

*Actor:* Right. And the comparison with their hollow, triumphant self will do them in.

*Professor:* Maybe. But this is tactics. Can't we talk strategy?

*Actor:* Of course we can. After all, if we have the strategy and tactics right we'll always win.

*Director:* Not if we don't have the needed strength.

*Actor:* We tailor the strategy to suit our strength.

*Professor:* But shouldn't we tailor the tactics and leave the strategy intact?

*Actor:* You have to be relatively strong for that.

*Director:* Let's look at a general example. What's a strategy for happiness?

*Actor:* To do all you do the best you can.

*Director:* And you, the actor, you act the best you can—and this makes you happy?

*Actor:* It does.

*Director:* But if you're not strong enough to act very well?

*Actor:* I'm really no good? I have to change what I do.

*Professor:* But we're saying that's a tactical change. Your strategy remains intact. You still want to do the best you can do. You're just going to change what you do.

*Actor:* That's true enough. And that makes the change sound less severe.

*Director:* But tell us. If your strategy is as you describe, when would you ever change it?

*Actor:* You have a point. Never.

*Director:* Then maybe it's not a strategy.

*Actor:* Why not?

*Director:* Because every strategy can be changed. You seem to be talking about some sort of natural law, something that always endures.

*Professor:* Yes. And there's an example we should consider. It takes us once more to war. Say you're a saboteur-spy, and you find yourself employed in logistics by the enemy. Would you want to be as good at logistics as you can? Or would you undermine the effort?

*Actor:* I'm not sure that's a good example.

*Professor:* Why not?

*Actor:* Because you're not really doing logistics. You're engaged in sabotage. So you want to be the best saboteur you can be. And that, at some point, involves not doing logistics very well.

*Director:* Is that how it is with everything?

*Actor:* What do you mean?

*Director:* I mean, you need to know what you really are, what you're really about.

*Actor:* Yes, of course.

*Director:* And as long as you do that thing well, you're... what?

*Actor:* Happy.

*Director:* Professor, what do you think?

*Professor:* If you know you're a philosopher, for instance, and you find yourself acting a different role on stage, so to speak; as long as you're the best philosopher you can be, it doesn't matter how well you perform.

*Actor:* Are you referring to me? I'm an actor, not a philosopher, Professor.

*Professor:* You're not willing to work undercover?

*Actor:* Of course not. I want to be what I am, for everyone to see.

## 79

*Director:* You want others to know you for what you are.

*Actor:* Yes.

*Director:* Then what an odd choice of profession you've made.

*Actor:* Why?

*Director:* You're known for your roles, not who you are. Or will you tell us you are your roles? After all, you spend most of your life in character. Don't you?

*Actor:* I want others to know me as an actor, a good actor. It's as simple as that.

*Professor:* But you separate your roles from yourself?

*Actor:* Well, of course. There's a part of me that isn't the role.

*Professor:* Director, is there a part of you that isn't a philosopher?

*Director:* No, Professor, there isn't. I'm philosopher through and through. And you?

*Professor:* I, too, am philosopher through and through. Actor, wouldn't you like to be something through and through?

*Actor:* I have to admit, that's appealing.

*Director:* Can you be an actor through and through?

*Actor:* Now that I think of it, I can.

*Director:* How?

*Actor:* Acting is my job, yes. But I also act outside my professional roles.

*Director:* What do you mean?

*Actor:* I act in my private life, too.

*Director:* What roles do you adopt?

*Actor:* You want the honest truth?

*Director:* You know I do.

*Actor:* I adopt roles I think will please.

*Director:* That's a remarkable confession. You're a people pleaser at heart?

*Actor:* I am. But it doesn't matter. Because I only act in private so long before I'm back on the job.

*Director:* Are you acting here with us today?

*Actor:* That's the funny thing. I'm not, at least not much.

*Director:* Why do you think that is?

*Actor:* Honestly? I think it's because of philosophy.

*Professor:* Because you're in the company of philosophers?

*Actor:* Yes. You're pleased by truth, whatever the truth might be. And that's a relief.

*Professor:* Then you should spend more time with philosophers, and maybe become one yourself.

*Actor:* But here I must be honest with you. I'm not always pleased by truth.

*Director:* When are you not pleased?

*Actor:* When I know I did a poor job. I still hope the reviews will be good.

*Director:* You're not relieved by honest reviews?

*Actor:* No, I'm not. Maybe a part of me, in a sense, yes. But overall? I'm not.

*Director:* Would you like to be relieved by honest reviews?

*Actor:* No. I'd like to have good reviews for jobs well done.

*Director:* Professor, do your students fill out evaluations of your performance at the end of a course?

*Professor:* They do. And sometimes I learn from them.

*Director:* Do you learn from good reviews?

*Professor:* Sometimes. But I more often learn from the critical.

*Director:* What makes a critical review good?

*Professor:* It clearly explains where I've gone wrong.

*Director:* Do you like to learn where you've gone wrong?

*Professor:* I do.

*Director:* Actor, can't you learn in this way from your critical reviews?

*Actor:* I can.

*Director:* Aren't you pleased to learn?

*Actor:* Not really.

*Director:* What's the difference between you two, Professor and Actor? Why is one pleased to learn while the other is not?

*Actor:* Professor isn't in the public eye. No one really sees his reviews. My reviews are broadcast far and wide.

*Director:* You'd prefer private reviews?

*Actor:* I really would.

*Professor:* But that's the price you pay for fame. Nothing private.

*Actor:* If I could make a living from acting, with no fame, I would.

*Director:* What would be the point?

*Actor:* I love to act.

*Director:* Is that the test of a pure love? You can do without the fame?

*Actor:* I think it is. You, Director, love to philosophize but have no fame. Your love for philosophy is pure.

*Professor:* Yes, but he has a reputation. And when that reputation goes far and wide, doesn't that amount to fame?

*Actor:* I think there's a difference.

*Professor:* Oh? Please tell us what it is.

*Actor:* You can have a reputation among a handful of people, far and wide or not. You can't have fame with just a few.

*Director:* What's the basic idea of fame?

*Actor:* Everyone knows your name and something about you.

*Director:* And what's the basic idea of reputation?

*Actor:* You're known for a certain quality.

*Director:* Would you rather have reputation or fame?

*Actor:* A good reputation or fair fame? I'd want both.

*Director:* And you Professor?

*Professor:* I'd choose good reputation.

*Director:* Who would choose fair fame over good reputation?

*Actor:* Many, Director. A good reputation is hard to achieve.

*Director:* And fame isn't?

*Actor:* What can I say? It's easier to win.

*Professor:* Easier?

*Actor:* It can be, and often is—won in a moment.

### 80

*Director:* What makes a reputation good? What's the idea?

*Actor:* If you're known for anything that's good, your reputation is good.

*Director:* So if I'm known for my good haircut, my reputation is good?

*Actor:* Well, you're being ridiculous.

*Director:* Am I? What if I'm known for my good physique? Ridiculous then?

*Actor:* Good reputations are built on character, not appearance.

*Director:* What's the idea of character?

*Actor:* Character is a habitual way of doing things.

*Director:* So if I'm honest by habit my character is good?

*Actor:* Yes.

*Director:* When we do something by habit, how do we do it?

*Actor:* I don't understand what you mean.

*Director:* I mean this—do we do it unthinkingly?

*Actor:* I don't know I'd say that.

*Director:* Why not?

*Actor:* Because it makes little of the honest heart.

*Director:* The heart that's honest out of habit.

*Actor:* You want to make habit sound like a little thing.

*Director:* No, I want to understand character. You said it's a habitual way of doing things. What's the opposite of habit?

*Actor:* Active choice.

*Director:* Would you rather be known for habit, or would you rather be known for active choice?

*Actor:* Active choice.

*Director:* Why?

*Actor:* Because active choice suggests that you're aware.

*Director:* Aware of what?

*Actor:* What you're doing.

*Director:* Do you want a reputation for being aware of what you're doing?

*Actor:* Of course I do.

*Director:* Then you don't want a reputation of doing things out of habit.

*Professor:* Actor, you don't seem pleased by this.

*Actor:* That's because good habit is good.

*Professor:* And bad habit is bad.

*Actor:* Of course.

*Director:* Let's look at an example. Are there times when it's good to forgive?

*Actor:* No doubt.

*Director:* But is it always good to forgive?

*Actor:* People are divided on that.

*Director:* Let's say you belong, out of habit, to those who always forgive. What if there comes a time when it wouldn't be good to forgive?

*Actor:* I'd have to break the habit.

*Director:* And if you were lazy?

*Actor:* What do you mean?

*Director:* Doesn't it take effort to break a habit?

*Actor:* Yes, it does.

*Director:* So if you were lazy, you might not break it.

*Actor:* True.

*Director:* Does always operating out of habit induce a certain sort of laziness?

*Actor:* It does.

*Director:* Now, you said character is a habitual way of doing things. Is character a lazy thing?

*Actor:* Of course not.

*Director:* What is it?

*Actor:* Making good choices time after time.

*Director:* So we want a reputation for good choices.

*Actor:* Yes.

*Director:* Can we be famous for good choices?

*Actor:* Definitely.

*Director:* Can we live in obscurity and be happy for the good choices we make?

*Actor:* Without a doubt.

*Director:* Are good choices always good?

*Actor:* By definition, yes.

*Director:* Professor, what do you think?

*Professor:* There can be two senses of 'good'.

*Director:* What's the first sense?

*Professor:* Good as in popularly approved.

*Director:* And the second sense?

*Professor:* Good in the true sense, in the proper idea of good.

*Director:* And that good is always good?

*Professor:* Yes.

*Director:* How do we know the always good?

*Professor:* We test it over time.

*Director:* So there's no love at first sight for the good?

*Professor:* There might be, but you still must test it over time.

*Director:* Isn't that how it is for reputation?

*Professor:* Of course. You must test it over time.

*Director:* So if someone tells you so-and-so's reputation is bad, you'd want to know if that reflects the truth?

*Professor:* I would.

*Director:* And it's the same if the reputation is good?

*Professor:* I'd want to know if the reputation is true.

### 81

*Director:* Now, we'd never say, "I want to know if the fame is true." Would we?

*Professor:* No, we wouldn't say that.

*Director:* Fame is or it isn't. But reputation is otherwise. Reputation can be true or false.

*Professor:* That puts it well.

*Actor:* But you can be famous for having a certain reputation, true or not.

*Professor:* So someone who's honest can be famous for having a reputation as a terrific liar?

*Actor:* Why not?

*Professor:* How would he or she get this reputation? It doesn't make sense.

*Actor:* They might have a sharp wit. Sharp wits often aren't believed, especially when sarcasm or irony are in play.

*Director:* What makes a wit sharp?

*Actor:* The clever use of words.

*Director:* And cleverness wins fame.

*Actor:* It can, yes.

*Director:* What's the idea of cleverness?

*Actor:* It's the unusual voicing of an unexpected truth.

*Director:* That sounds like a good reason to be famous, to me.

*Professor:* Yes, but it's that unusual voicing that trips them up.

*Actor:* What do you mean?

*Professor:* Instead of focusing on the simple statement of the truth, the clever ones are bent on making a name for themselves. As a result, they often distort the truth.

*Director:* And they win fame for their distorted truth?

*Professor:* Often times, yes.

*Director:* Well, that's no good. So it's better to be truthful than clever.

*Professor:* Yes, though truth doesn't win the same fame.

*Director:* I suspect if you were truthful about the right things, you might win more fame.

*Actor:* What makes a thing 'right'?

*Director:* It's something people really want to know.

*Actor:* The unvarnished truth?

*Director:* Yes, the honest plain truth.

*Actor:* When would people not want that?

*Director:* When they prefer to be entertained.

*Actor:* What's the idea of entertainment?

*Director:* That's a funny thing for an actor to ask.

*Actor:* Funny or not, what is it?

*Director:* It's something that provides amusement or enjoyment.

*Actor:* What's the difference between amusement and enjoyment?

*Director:* Maybe it's best to give an example. I can enjoy a hot shower. But I wouldn't say it amuses me. Would I?

*Actor:* No, you wouldn't.

*Director:* So what's the difference?

*Actor:* I'll answer by giving another example. I can enjoy a fine sunset, but I wouldn't say I'm amused by the sun.

*Professor:* Yes, but what about the opposite? Can you ever say you can be amused but not enjoy?

*Actor:* No, I don't think you can.

*Professor:* So enjoyment is the broader category.

*Actor:* Yes. Then we'll say entertainment is something that provides enjoyment.

*Director:* Tell us, Actor. What's the difference between entertaining yourself or being entertained?

*Actor:* Let's stick with examples. I might entertain myself by reading a book. Or I might be entertained by clever people at a party.

*Professor:* But with a book it's the author who entertains.

*Actor:* Okay. So let's say I entertain myself by writing the book. How's that?

*Director:* I think that's better. But now I want to know if we can be entertained by the honest plain truth.

*Actor:* I think the answer is yes.

*Director:* That doesn't cheapen the truth?

*Actor:* Truth is never cheap.

*Professor:* Not even if people are amused by the truth?

*Actor:* There's something wrong with them.

*Professor:* What's wrong?

*Actor:* Truth shouldn't be amusing.

*Professor:* Truth is inherently serious?

*Actor:* Of course it is.

*Professor:* Because truth is moral?

*Actor:* Our relation to truth is moral.

*Professor:* And there's nothing entertaining about the moral.

*Director:* I can think of something, something close to Actor's heart.

*Actor:* What?

*Director:* I once saw you in a film where you were an honest fool. You went about speaking truth at inopportune moments. And everyone laughed.

*Actor:* Yes, but that's just a film.

*Director:* It wouldn't be funny in real life?

*Professor:* I think it would. Am I immoral?

*Actor:* Okay, you might have a point.

*Professor:* So truth can be funny. Can integrity?

*Director:* I think it can.

*Actor:* How?

*Director:* Integrity drives your telling the truth in the film. Without your integrity, we wouldn't have as much fun.

*Actor:* Yes, but that's a comedy. How about in real life? There's something tragic about being laughed at for integrity and truth.

*Director:* And yet your film was very popular. You even won an award.

*Professor:* That shows people want to laugh at integrity and truth. The film gives them license.

*Director:* Is there any idea we can't laugh at given the proper setting?

*Professor:* No.

*Actor:* But what makes the setting proper?

*Director:* When no one gets hurt.

### 82

*Actor:* Yes! That's exactly it. No one got hurt by the film.

*Professor:* But sometimes laughter should hurt.

*Actor:* When?

*Professor:* When we expose practicing deceivers.

*Actor:* We laugh at them, and then the pain of the laughter compels them to stop? I think it's the exposure that compels them to stop. The laughter is just gravy.

*Professor:* But can't laughter be just punishment?

*Actor:* For a minor deceit? Sure.

*Director:* But is laughter all that reliable a punishment?

*Professor:* Why wouldn't it be?

*Director:* Some are affected by it more than others.

*Actor:* I agree. And that makes Professor's punishment-by-laughter an unreliable idea.

*Director:* Because you can't be sure what effect the laughter will have. But that makes me wonder.

*Actor:* What are you wondering?

*Director:* I wonder about the truth. Truth might have one effect on someone, and it might have another effect on another. Is truth unreliable?

*Actor:* Of course not.

*Director:* What makes something unreliable?

*Professor:* I know what you want us to say.

*Director:* What do I want us to say?

*Professor:* Combination.

*Director:* So when you combine laughter with force for good, that's unreliable? Sometimes there will be good, and sometimes not?

*Professor:* Well?

*Actor:* I think that's exactly right.

*Director:* What if we just combine laughter with force?

*Actor:* No mention of good? Maybe that's a better idea.

*Professor:* But an idea that says what?

*Actor:* Oh, who cares? Not everyone will feel the force.

*Professor:* Who doesn't feel the force of laughter?

*Actor:* You tell me.

*Professor:* Someone with something wrong with them.

*Director:* So someone with something wrong with them wouldn't feel compelled by laughter to change their ways, those ways being mocked?

*Professor:* Precisely.

*Actor:* I don't know. There's courage in standing up to laughter. It's something to admire.

*Professor:* Not when the one standing up is a sociopath.

*Actor:* I never really understood what that word means.

*Director:* Let me venture a definition. A sociopath is anyone who makes ideas seem unreliable.

*Professor:* Then philosophers are sociopaths?

*Actor:* That can't be right. You two are as far from being that as anyone I know.

*Director:* What makes you say that?

*Actor:* You both have what I'd call a philosophical conscience.

*Professor:* He has a point.

*Director:* And what does that conscience dictate?

*Actor:* For our purposes today? That ideas should serve people, or they're bad.

*Director:* They should do people well.

*Actor:* Exactly.

*Director:* Even bad people?

*Actor:* The ideas should give them what they deserve.

*Director:* I see. And if they don't?

*Actor:* The ideas are bad.

*Director:* And it's up to the philosopher to say which is which.

*Actor:* That's what philosophers do.

*Director:* Do philosophers laugh at the bad?

*Actor:* Bad people? Sometimes.

*Director:* Why not always?

*Actor:* Because sometimes they laugh at the ideas instead.

*Director:* Are you sure we can distinguish between the person and their ideas?

*Actor:* I do. All healthy people do.

*Director:* Why?

*Actor:* Because how could anyone ever change an idea if the idea weren't different than them?

*Professor:* He has a good point.

*Director:* He does. But let's get back to laughter. What kind of humor do the bad deserve?

*Actor:* Harsh humor.

*Director:* And the good?

*Actor:* Something chiding, gentle.

*Director:* To each their own.

*Actor:* Yes, there's a sort of proportion here.

*Director:* Proportion? I suppose we can say that. But I'd rather speak of the fitting. Regardless, these things are matters of justice. Can we ever do anything right without a sense of justice?

*Actor:* I don't think we can.

*Director:* We can never do anything right without a sense of what's good. That's much the same thing?

*Actor:* Yes.

*Director:* Okay. But I'm having trouble here.

*Actor:* What trouble?

*Director:* It's a question of reduction again.

*Actor:* What do you want to reduce?

*Director:* Right to good. After all, can't we say the right is good?

*Actor:* Of course we can. But we can also say the good is right.

*Director:* Yes. Does that mean that they're the same? Two different words that mean the same thing?

*Professor:* No. A gentle summertime breeze is good. We wouldn't say it's right.

*Director:* Hmm. Yes. Actor, what do you think?

*Actor:* There's nothing just about a summertime breeze.

*Director:* Not even if it's just right considering the temperature?

*Actor:* Just right. There's a lot we can say about being just right.

*Director:* A joke might be just right in bite.

*Actor:* True. And a meal could be seasoned just right in spice.

*Director:* Just right means good.

*Actor:* But right alone doesn't.

*Director:* Really? So we wouldn't say an artist got your portrait right?

*Actor:* No, I suppose we would say that.

*Director:* And to say the artist got it just right makes no difference?

*Actor:* None at all, except in emphasis.

*Director:* And if we say the artist painted a good portrait of you?

*Actor:* That's different.

*Director:* How?

*Actor:* Just right is better than good.

*Director:* Because just right means exactly so.

*Actor:* Yes. Good is an approximation. 'The meal was good' says less than 'the meal was just right'.

*Director:* Just right is perfect?

*Actor:* And good is only more or less good.

### 83

*Director:* Now I feel I have to question all we've said about good.

*Actor:* Why? There are two ideas. Good, and perfect.

*Director:* But I doubt this idea of perfection.

*Actor:* Why would you?

*Director:* Because nothing is perfect in this world.

*Actor*: But we want something greater than good.

*Director*: Then we can say, for instance, my film was good but yours was great.

*Actor*: But you know what we all want.

*Director*: Do I? What do we want?

*Actor*: Not to be good. Not to be better. But to be best.

*Director*: So there is no perfect, just closer to perfect than the rest.

*Actor*: Exactly.

*Director*: But this creates all kinds of trouble.

*Actor*: How so?

*Director*: Is the only true success being the best?

*Actor*: Well, you can be very good or even great, but not the best. There's success in that.

*Director*: Then why try for best? Why not be content with great?

*Actor*: Because excellence in itself is worthwhile.

*Director*: And the more excellence the better.

*Actor*: Of course.

*Director*: But I still have my doubts.

*Actor*: What doubts?

*Director*: Why should we compete?

*Actor*: Compete to be the best?

*Director*: Yes. Why?

*Actor*: Because competition brings out excellence.

*Director*: But why not be best at what only you can do?

*Actor*: No competition?

*Director*: No competition.

*Actor*: You just have to find your niche?

*Director*: You have to find where you excel.

*Actor*: But what if you excel where others excel?

*Director*: Then you haven't found your thing.

*Actor*: Your thing. Is that an idea? The idea of the thing?

*Director*: Yes, it's an idea.

*Professor*: What's your thing, Director?

*Director:* Philosophy.

*Professor:* But philosophy is my thing, too. Do we compete?

*Director:* No, philosophers don't compete.

*Professor:* My students compete.

*Director:* The ones who do aren't philosophers.

*Actor:* Why not?

*Director:* Philosophers collaborate.

*Actor:* In getting at truth? But they all say such different things.

*Director:* Truth is multifaceted.

*Actor:* So they approach truth through the facets they face?

*Director:* Yes.

*Actor:* And each philosopher has a different view?

*Director:* That's right.

*Actor:* Then what does it mean to train a student?

*Director:* We should ask Professor.

*Professor:* We show the student our view. And then we chase them away.

*Actor:* Toward their own view?

*Professor:* Toward their own view.

*Actor:* What if they come back?

*Professor:* We chase them away again.

*Actor:* And what if you die, and then they come back?

*Professor:* They're doomed, unless some other philosopher sees what's happening and takes up the cause.

*Actor:* The cause? You mean chasing them away.

*Professor:* Every philosopher wants every one else to see things on their own.

*Actor:* I believe you. But why?

*Professor:* Because that's what's needed to fight the fight.

*Actor:* What fight?

*Professor:* Director?

*Director:* The fight, Actor, is against a terrible foe.

*Actor:* What foe?

*Director:* The false idea.

*Actor:* You say it as if there's only one.

*Director:* And there is. It has to do with the good.

*Actor:* How did I know you'd say that?

*Director:* You know because you've been paying attention.

*Actor:* Let me guess. The false idea leads you away from the good.

*Director:* Yes.

*Actor:* But there are millions of false ideas!

*Director:* But they are all, in what they do—one.

## 84

*Professor:* Those with false ideas all recoil from the good.

*Actor:* The good drives them away?

*Professor:* Yes.

*Actor:* Why?

*Professor:* I really don't know. But I do know these people often spout outrageous ideas as they flee.

*Actor:* So, Director, your fight is against the outrageous?

*Director:* Actually, I leave that to others. My fight is against the subtle.

*Actor:* Professor, is that your fight, too?

*Professor:* It is.

*Actor:* Why don't you two fight the outrageous?

*Professor:* There are others better suited for that.

*Actor:* What makes you suited to fight the subtle?

*Professor:* We're willing to take them seriously.

*Actor:* That's what it takes to fight them? Seriousness?

*Professor:* You have to beat them at their own game.

*Director:* Yes, but you can do that without being serious.

*Actor:* How does that work?

*Director:* You make your case to them in full subtlety. Then you let them suspect you're joking.

*Actor:* What kind of joke is that?

*Director:* One that might startle them into changing their ways.

*Actor:* What if it only makes them worse?

*Director:* Then there's probably nothing anyone can do.

*Actor:* Why not take them completely seriously?

*Director:* That's what they want.

*Actor:* So you give your enemies what seems to be what they want, but isn't.

*Director:* Yes. But I wouldn't say they're the enemy. Their ideas are the enemies.

*Actor:* I thought there was only one false idea.

*Director:* One false idea with countless variations.

*Actor:* And each philosopher best attacks certain variations.

*Director:* Yes.

*Actor:* Professor?

*Professor:* I agree about the variations.

*Actor:* But can't philosophers attack any variation they encounter?

*Professor:* Yes, but they're only best at some.

*Actor:* But let's be more clear. What are we talking about? Prejudices?

*Professor:* By and large, yes.

*Actor:* So we're saying philosophers should attack the prejudices of their time and place.

*Professor:* Which is to say, the prejudices they know best. And there are many times and places in any given time and place.

*Actor:* But a prejudice is a false idea?

*Professor:* None more false.

*Actor:* How do we attack a prejudice?

*Professor:* Ah, that's the art of philosophy.

*Actor:* I thought philosophy was science.

*Professor:* Science is science. Philosophy is an art.

*Actor:* So what's the art of attacking prejudice?

*Professor:* You tailor your attack to each individual idea.

*Actor:* To each person, you mean.

*Professor:* As Director said, we attack the idea, not the person.

*Actor:* But a person holds the idea.

*Professor:* Alright, you have a point. We tailor the attack to the idea and its holder.

*Actor:* In order to get them to let go.

*Professor:* Yes.

*Actor:* And when they let go?

*Professor:* They're free to take up a true idea.

### 85

*Actor:* Some will take up philosophy?

*Professor:* Some will, yes.

*Actor:* The better ones?

*Professor:* Philosophy is no better than any true idea.

*Actor:* You didn't quite answer my question. But, Director, do you believe that about philosophy?

*Director:* It's not a matter of belief.

*Actor:* Okay, but how can we know one idea is better than another?

*Director:* True ideas are all equally good.

*Actor:* Truth equalizes things?

*Director:* You put that well.

*Actor:* But what about false ideas? Are they all equally bad?

*Professor:* No, some are worse than others.

*Actor:* Then why aren't some true ideas better than others?

*Professor:* Because truth is privileged here.

*Actor:* Here?

*Professor:* Among the three of us. Not all people privilege truth.

*Actor:* They think some truths are better than others?

*Professor:* They do. And that's a mistake.

*Actor:* What happens to those who make the mistake?

*Professor:* Their ideas about truth carry them away. They think some truths are higher than others. And off they fly, ignoring what they consider to be the baser truths.

*Actor:* And when you ignore those truths?

*Professor:* Your foundation cracks.

*Actor:* What should we call their 'baser truths'?

*Professor:* The fundamentals, without which no higher truth can be.

*Actor:* But didn't you just say it's a mistake to think some truths are higher than others?

*Professor:* And it is. Truth is always on a level field with truth.

*Actor:* Then why speak of fundamental truth? Why speak of higher truths?

*Professor:* Because not everyone can see how truly equal truth is.

*Actor:* So you'd encourage them in a lie? That some truths are more important than others?

*Director:* Professor, something isn't right. So let's consider an example. It's true that ants are small. It's true that someone loves me. Which truth is higher, is more important?

*Professor:* Why do you think higher is more important? Love is a fundamental truth. It's high and low at once.

*Actor:* And that's what makes it important?

*Professor:* Yes. But ability to judge what's important is equally important with the important.

*Actor:* So knowing ants are small is as important as love?

*Professor:* Yes.

*Actor:* I think you're playing a game.

*Professor:* How can we know what's great if we don't know what's small?

*Director:* And it's good to know these things?

*Professor:* Yes.

*Actor:* Oh, I'm tired of the good.

*Director:* Why?

*Actor:* Because it's the answer for everything!

*Professor:* It might not be the answer, but it's a sure guide.

*Actor:* How so?

*Professor:* Well, which would you prefer? Good love or bad?

*Actor:* Bad love isn't love.

*Professor:* Tell that to those in the midst of it.

*Actor:* Okay. I prefer good love to bad.

*Professor:* When we prefer something, what do we usually say?

*Actor:* I don't know what you're after.

*Professor:* Don't we say, "I'd take this over that"?

*Actor:* Sure we do.

*Professor:* Whatever is over something is higher, no?

*Actor:* True.

*Professor:* And whatever is beneath something is lower.

*Actor:* Yes. What's the point?

*Professor:* There's a bias in our language for the higher. But we said love, something I think all of us would take, is fundamental—it's higher and lower at once.

*Actor:* Love is profound.

*Professor:* Is the good profound?

*Actor:* It's among the highest things there are. But it's also fundamental. So, yes, I'd say it's profound.

*Professor:* 'Among the highest'?

*Actor:* Love is equal to the good.

*Professor:* So love and goodness differ?

*Actor:* Of course they do. So don't banish love from your class.

*Professor:* I'm not sure why they differ as a matter 'of course'.

*Actor:* When love is true it can take you beyond the good.

*Professor:* What's beyond the good? The bad?

*Actor:* No, the supra-good.

*Professor:* The better?

*Actor:* No, the best.

*Director:* Is love the only thing that goes beyond the good?

*Actor:* The only thing I know. And you?

*Director:* It's hard to say.

*Actor:* Hard to say because you know the truth and this truth is hard? Or hard to say because you don't know?

*Director:* I don't know what it means to go beyond the good.

*Actor:* It means you're willing to sacrifice the good for that which goes beyond.

*Director:* So you'd be willing to sacrifice good for love.

*Actor:* I would.

*Professor:* That's destructive, you know.

*Actor:* Destructive of what?

*Professor:* Potentially? Everything you hold to be good.

*Actor:* Then that's the price I pay.

### 86

*Director:* To love is to sacrifice all?

*Actor:* No doubt. Don't you know? You have to feed the all consuming flame.

*Director:* So love can consume the good.

*Actor:* Well, you make it sound so bad.

*Director:* Love can't consume the good?

*Actor:* Love and the good are different things.

*Director:* So you can have love and good. And you can have love and no good. Or you can have good and no love.

*Actor:* Yes.

*Director:* Which is best?

*Actor:* Love and good.

*Director:* Professor?

*Professor:* Love and good is best.

*Director:* What's second best? Love and no good, or good and no love?

*Actor:* Love and no good.

*Professor:* Good and no love.

*Director:* We have a real difference of opinion here. Professor, why do you prefer good?

*Professor:* Because good is what makes us whole.

*Director:* Actor? Why do you prefer love?

*Actor:* Because love makes us whole!

*Director:* Are we sure good and love are different things?

*Professor:* Positive.

*Actor:* Yes. But are you sure, Director?

*Director:* Well, since I'm sure love can be bad....

*Actor:* I'm not so sure you actually believe that. What you're calling bad love is actually infatuation.

*Professor:* What is infatuation?

*Actor:* Unrequited love.

*Director:* You mean it's not fully fledged.

*Actor:* Fully fledged love is mutual.

*Director:* To be mutual the lovers must be at the right time and place?

*Actor:* What do you mean?

*Director:* Maybe I can explain by telling you what I've heard from the infatuated I've known. If only the time and place were right, they say, there would be love.

*Actor:* Yes, I do think they think something like that.

*Director:* And what does it mean? They believe love isn't absolute? It depends on time and place? On circumstance, in other words?

*Actor:* You have a point about the infatuated. But that's not what I like to say.

*Professor:* What do you say?

*Director:* I think he says love is absolute.

*Actor:* The one you're meant to love is the one you're meant to love. Absolutely.

*Professor:* And what of circumstance?

*Actor:* Love doesn't depend on it. It depends on love.

*Professor:* What an idea! Circumstance subservient to love!

*Actor:* It makes good sense.

*Director:* Would you say that about the good?

*Actor:* Circumstance is subservient to the good? I would.

*Professor:* Then circumstance is simply the means to an end, be it goodness or love.

*Actor:* Yes.

*Professor:* And the end justifies the means.

*Actor:* If the end is goodness or love? Yes.

*Director:* Didn't we say a good end needs good means?

*Actor:* We did. Good means are best. But let me tell you a secret. When it comes to goodness and love—there's quite a bit of play!

87

*Director:* Yes, but is there anything that justifies any means?

*Actor:* War for survival?

*Professor:* Survival at any cost? No matter how horrific the means?

*Actor:* No, you have a point. Sometimes it's best to lose.

*Director:* I'm surprised you'd say this.

*Actor:* Why?

*Director:* Because you like to win on stage and screen.

*Actor:* That's different.

*Director:* How?

*Actor:* No one dies.

*Professor:* Says the one who always gets the part.

*Actor:* I've been passed over before.

*Professor:* Did you want to die?

*Actor:* Yes. But I got over it.

*Professor:* How?

*Actor:* Success in the audition wasn't my highest idea.

*Professor:* What was your highest idea?

*Actor:* Finding the circumstances that were right for me.

*Professor:* You failed the audition because the circumstances weren't right?

*Actor:* Yes.

*Professor:* It wasn't because of your performance?

*Actor:* No.

*Professor:* I wish everyone could see it that way.

*Director:* Why?

*Professor:* We put too much blame on ourselves. If things don't go well, it's not always our fault. We simply must try again and hope circumstance favors.

*Director:* But what if things are our fault?

*Actor:* Who can say who's fault something is?

*Director:* Don't you know when you act poorly?

*Actor:* Well, of course.

*Director:* And when you do, it's your fault?

*Actor:* Not really. The one conducting the audition might have made me nervous. I might have been sick, had a bad cold. The chemistry with the one I auditioned with might have been bad. I could go on and on.

*Director:* Well, this is quite an idea. Circumstances are to blame.

*Actor:* What's wrong with that idea? They really are.

*Director:* Are circumstances to blame when you have success?

*Actor:* You don't blame when you have success.

*Director:* Excuse me. Do you praise circumstances when you have success?

*Actor:* Of course! You thank the stars for your good luck.

*Director:* Then what of the idea of merit?

*Actor:* There's merit in being prepared.

*Director:* What do you mean?

*Actor:* If the stars align but you're not prepared, you'll have no luck.

*Director:* So you prepare and then wait.

*Actor:* That's what all the best of us do.

*Director:* You've never heard of making your own luck?

*Actor:* I have. But I don't buy it.

*Director:* Why not?

*Actor:* Because that saying assumes we have more control than we do. Control is a terrible thing. It bends so many out of shape. And they're none the happier for it.

*Director:* Luck can be a terrible thing. It bends so many out of shape. And they're none the happier for it.

*Actor:* Yes, but if we prepare we have a chance to seize luck when it comes.

*Professor:* Director, that's true.

*Director:* It is. So this whole notion of conquering luck is false?

*Actor:* It can be done. But at a terrible cost.

*Professor:* It's best to let luck be what it will be, and to be prepared for when it's good.

*Director:* Shouldn't we be prepared for when it's bad?

*Professor:* We should always be prepared.

*Director:* So let luck be what it will be. Don't force it. But be prepared.

*Actor:* That's the way to happiness.

*Director:* Even if your luck is bad?

*Actor:* Bad luck is easier to swallow than personal failure.

*Professor:* It's true. Bad luck is no one's fault.

*Director:* But the greatly ambitious won't be satisfied with bad luck as their excuse.

*Actor:* It's not an excuse. It's a fact.

*Director:* Then the terribly ambitious won't be satisfied with that fact.

*Professor:* What can you do about facts?

*Director:* Strive to overcome them.

*Actor:* Yes, but all their striving makes them crazed.

*Director:* If crazed, then not happy?

*Actor:* Not happy at all—though they'll insist in dead earnest they are.

*Director:* Why is it important for them to seem happy?

*Actor:* Because they're cheating luck and paying the price. And they don't want to seem like they're cheating, so they act like they're not paying the price.

*Director:* Is it really cheating to work very hard? Who would agree? Some would say relying on luck is a sort of cheat.

*Actor:* Relying on luck is honest.

*Director:* Why?

*Actor:* Because luck affects us all.

*Director:* Clearly hard work doesn't affect us all.

*Actor:* But those who prepare for luck work hard, very hard.

*Director:* Then what's the difference?

*Actor:* Control. Haven't you heard that prayer? Give me the strength to change the things I can, and the wisdom to accept the things I can't.

*Director:* I think the prayer is a little different than that. But I take your point.

*Actor:* The point is that those who seek to control or overcome luck aren't wise.

*Director:* Because we can't change luck.

*Actor:* Luck is luck. You have to accept your luck and move on.

*Director:* Or else?

*Actor:* Things get bad.

88

*Director:* People don't take credit for the bad. But they often take credit for the good.

*Actor:* For good luck? You mean, if I'm a finalist for a part, and the other person falls and breaks a leg, and therefore I'm chosen—I might say it wasn't luck that got me the role. It was my talent.

*Director:* Yes. Doesn't that happen all the time?

*Actor:* Sure.

*Director:* What sort of person admits luck had a hand in their success?

*Actor:* An honest one.

*Director:* When does luck cross over to become destiny?

*Actor:* Ah, that's a good question. It happens when people believe in the idea of their luck.

*Director:* You mean they believe their luck isn't luck.

*Actor:* Exactly.

*Director:* What an odd belief. Why not just believe there's no such thing as luck?

*Actor:* You mean, things happen for a reason? Plenty of people think that.

*Director:* But isn't their belief a way of coping with bad luck? It leaves them searching for a silver lining to the cloud. Surely that's alright.

*Actor:* It's great to make the most of bad luck. I think people should say, "I'll find a reason in this and make some good of the bad."

*Professor:* Yes, but you have to find the right reason. You have to have the right idea.

*Director:* And if you don't?

*Professor:* It's dangerous.

*Actor:* Dangerous?

*Professor:* Don't you know reasons can harm?

*Actor:* They can make you believe simple bad luck was your fault, if that's what you mean.

*Professor:* That is what I mean. Certain people never learn to recognize luck as luck. And they think things will go better if only they try that much harder.

*Actor:* I know what you're talking about. It becomes an obsession. They put on blinders and try and try and try again.

*Director:* What's wrong with blinders?

*Actor:* You smile. But I'll tell you what's wrong. In this life we're meant to see—all we can see.

### 89

*Director:* Well, we've been here a while. We'd better leave a big tip.

*Actor:* Here, give me the check. It's on me.

*Professor:* No, we'll split it three ways.

*Actor:* Alright. But I'll leave the tip.

*Director:* He wants to impress the waitress.

*Professor:* He did that just by showing up.

*Director:* Yes, but he has a problem.

*Actor:* What problem?

*Director:* The problem with being famous. Everyone expects something good from you.

*Actor:* And that makes me expect good of myself.

*Professor:* You just don't want to let anyone down.

*Actor:* If good comes of that fear, so what?

*Director:* I thought you'd say you love your fans, and the love brings out the good.

*Actor:* Of course it does. But sometimes you need a little fear when the love is running low.

*Director:* Like when your fans don't love you but an idea of you?

*Actor:* You like to make that point. Well, it's true—those who don't know me love the idea.

*Director:* And you seek to shape the idea.

*Actor:* Of course.

*Professor:* That's what publicists and marketers do.

*Actor:* Yes, but they work with what I give them. I do interviews, make public appearances, and so much more.

*Director:* I always wonder when people tack on 'and so much more' if there really is so much more.

*Actor:* Follow me around a while and see.

*Director:* Much as I'd like to, I have to make it to the office at some point today.

*Professor:* Yes, and class starts soon.

*Actor:* Do you mind if I sit in?

*Professor:* You'll distract the students.

*Actor:* Maybe that will stir things up.

*Professor:* Alright. You're more than welcome to come. They never knew their professor was so cool.

*Director:* You don't want to come to work with me? You'll stir up the team.

*Actor:* I think it's likely you stir them up plenty on your own.

*Director:* Yes, but I'm not sure they think I'm cool.

*Actor:* You're beyond cool.

*Director:* What's beyond cool?

*Actor:* Being a philosopher.

*Director:* Now I think you're teasing me.

*Actor:* You can use a little of that.

*Director:* What can you use?

*Actor:* Some inspiration.

*Director:* Why?

*Actor:* I have an audition tomorrow.

*Director:* I didn't think people at your level auditioned. What's the part?

*Actor:* A man who witnesses a crime by someone he knows.

*Director:* Let me guess. He can't simply turn them in.

*Actor:* No, he can't. He's involved in a complex web of relationships that leave him no easy choice. And here's the twist. He's in love with the criminal.

*Director:* That's a fairly standard twist.

*Actor:* Yes, but I want to change the script. I want there to be two criminals, and he's in love with them both.

*Professor:* Will they let you change the script?

*Actor:* I'm going to bring what I wrote. I need to put the finishing touches on it tonight.

*Professor:* You rewrote the whole script?

*Actor:* No, just the part I'll audition tomorrow.

*Director:* Have you ever done something like this before?

*Actor:* I haven't. And I have no idea how it will go over.

*Professor:* Maybe you act their version first and then you act yours.

*Actor:* I thought of that. But I want to focus on my vision.

*Director:* What's your vision?

*Actor:* That love isn't limited to the One. There can be Two, or More.

*Professor:* Some people will want to hear that. But most? I don't know, Actor.

*Director:* Do you want it to be an art film?

*Actor:* Art film. The name for unpopular projects.

*Director:* Well, if you want to be popular you need to use popular ideas. The One of love is among the most popular.

*Professor:* Then how can his 'art' ever change people's opinions?

*Director:* If he really wants to take people from the One to the Two and beyond? I don't know. But I have another question.

### 90

*Actor:* What question?

*Director:* Who's putting you up to this?

*Actor:* No one.

*Director:* I don't believe you.

*Actor:* Well, there is... someone.

*Director:* Someone you love who holds this idea of beyond the One?

*Actor:* Yes.

*Director:* But you only love this one? I mean, you don't currently love anyone else?

*Actor:* I'm in love with her.

*Director:* And she, she loves others, too?

*Actor:* Well....

*Professor:* He's got it bad.

*Director:* Yes. So, Artist, what are you going to do?

*Actor:* Win her over wholly to me.

*Director:* How?

*Actor:* I think she's confused.

*Director:* She really only loves you? So let me guess. You're going to make a film that compels her to see the truth.

*Actor:* Alright, you figured it out. The One will win in the end in my script. That's why people will like the film.

*Director:* You'll go from the unconventional to the conventional. What will drive your character that way?

*Actor:* Unconventional love isn't enough.

*Director:* What makes him realize that?

*Actor:* He's not happy.

*Director:* And your film will make your real world love know she's unhappy?

*Actor:* That's the idea.

*Professor:* But what if your love really is happy, despite what you'd prefer? And if she is, she's managed that in the face of convention. Do you know how hard it is to be happy when you go against convention? And what will you do? Make a conventional film against her?

*Actor:* But if she's happy, she just won't like the film; and if she's unhappy, she will.

*Professor:* So you're hoping she's unhappy.

*Actor:* I guess I am.

*Director:* Actor, do you really believe people don't know if they're happy or unhappy?

*Actor:* I think some people lie to themselves.

*Director:* And your film will help expose that lie.

*Actor:* Yes.

*Professor:* But why go to all the trouble? Why not just talk to her in person, heart to heart?

*Actor:* I tried. It didn't work.

*Professor:* Then you need to walk away.

### 91

*Director:* Or maybe you could switch ideas.

*Actor:* Ha!

*Director:* Why do you laugh?

*Actor:* My idea of love is who I am!

*Director:* And yet you want her to change who she is for you. Or don't you think her idea of love is who she is?

*Actor:* That's exactly the point! It's not who she is.

*Director:* How do you know? Have you seen her when she's who she is?

*Actor:* When we're alone, yes.

*Director:* You want her to be how she is when she's alone with you, all the time.

*Actor:* Yes.

*Director:* But she can't or won't.

*Actor:* Won't.

*Director:* How do you know it's not because she can't?

*Actor:* I... just know.

*Director:* Professor, I'm very suspicious of these I-just-knows.

*Professor:* So am I. In this case it seems like some wishful thinking. But then again, I don't know the woman.

*Director:* A very good point. So, Actor, I think we've said all we can say about this. You've got a real battle of ideas on your hands. Good luck.

*Actor:* Good luck is all you can say?

*Director:* Good luck, and don't forget to leave the tip. But don't worry, things will work out fine.

*Actor:* How do you know?

*Director:* Your dedication to your career will carry you through. I know you'll take whatever bruised feelings you might have and put them to work in your craft.

*Actor:* And what about you?

*Director:* Me? I always have an eye out for love.

*Actor:* But you're not as serious about it as I am.

*Director:* You're younger and sometimes believe you can force the issue. Professor and I know you can't force love. And we look for the silver lining in all of our bad luck.

*Actor:* But I don't believe you two really think your luck is bad.

*Director:* What's our idea? Not the One or the Two, but the Zero?

*Professor:* I believe in no such thing.

*Director:* Nor do I. So, Actor, you should accept it when we tell you we have bad luck. Just as you should accept your own bad luck.

*Actor:* What bad luck?

*Director:* You really don't know?

*Professor:* Your love for this woman!

*Director:* I think he'll overcome his luck. He's resilient, a born actor.

*Actor:* Tease all you like. You made fair points that I need to digest.

*Director:* Are you going to offer your modified script?

*Actor:* Maybe that's not a great idea. I should want to win the part for what it is.

*Director:* Then I truly wish you good luck.

*Professor:* And now we have to get going. It's time for class.

*Director:* Yes, and business calls. We should do this again some time.

*Actor:* I agree. If I get the part I'll be in town for a few months.

*Director:* Then I hope you land that role.

*Actor:* Me, too. Do we have time to walk Director to the train?

*Professor:* If we hurry.

*Director:* Let's not end on a hurried note. Besides, I want to stop in the bookstore. There are so few of them left.

*Professor:* Yes, it's sad. But we have the best one in the city right here next door.

*Director:* How lucky for me.

*Actor:* Lucky? You picked the restaurant!

*Director:* It's always good luck if you can kill two birds with one stone.

*Professor:* What are you looking for in the bookstore, Director?

*Director:* A collection of Aesop's fables.

*Actor:* I didn't know you had an interest in that.

*Director:* I've taken to closing my team meetings with a fable.

*Actor:* Why?

*Director:* It's entertaining.

*Actor:* And there's a moral.

*Director:* No, not always. We often read the fable and then close by saying, 'And there's no moral here.'

*Actor:* What do your people think about that?

*Director:* They laugh every time.

*Actor:* And that's the point?

*Director:* We have enough tension at work. It's good to laugh. Do you laugh in class, Professor?

*Professor:* You've got me there. Not as much as we should.

*Actor:* Maybe today I'll help you laugh.

*Professor:* That would be a wonderful gift.

### 92

*Actor:* They say you should never come to another's home without a gift.

*Director:* And the philosophy department is Professor's home.

*Professor:* Hardly. I'm not the chair.

*Director:* But you somehow managed to become a full professor. I'd say it's your house as much as anyone's.

*Professor:* I like to think of myself as an outsider of sorts.

*Actor:* Oh, Professor. You're an insider all the way. Director, on the other hand, he's the outsider. He's a philosopher outside formal philosophy.

*Director:* And yet I see myself as an insider.

*Actor:* Now you're just trying to be contrary.

*Director:* No, really. I'm an insider in business.

*Professor:* I've never understood why you want to be that.

*Director:* It's because of the ideas.

*Actor:* What about the ideas?

*Director:* In our world, business ideas are strong. They have lots of force.

*Actor:* And what do you want to do with those ideas?

*Director:* Treat them as I would treat any idea.

*Actor:* Yes, but why them? Why not deal with other ideas?

*Director:* I fill a need.

*Professor:* What need?

*Director:* I'm not afraid of business ideas. Many are.

*Actor:* I'm not. Some of my films challenge those ideas.

*Director:* And we shouldn't underestimate the power of entertainment.

*Actor:* You can't even say that with a straight face.

*Professor:* But it's true, Actor. There's power in what you do.

*Actor:* Why do you think that is?

*Director:* Maybe it's because we're a nation of would-be entertainers.

*Actor:* I think it's true. But tell me, Director. What do entertainers know? What's their idea?

*Director:* Aside from fame or success? Oh, I don't know. I just see that they strive for a smile, a laugh, a frown, a tear.

*Professor:* Their idea is to move someone, whatever it takes.

*Director:* Move in a particular direction?

*Actor:* No. The idea is to move them, to get them started—then let them choose their direction.

*Director:* So what's the idea? To overcome inertia?

*Actor:* Yes, exactly that! Inertia is the enemy we fight with all our might. And I think all three of us fight this fight. And we'd all fight better and more if we could help each other know what to do.

*Professor:* Then we need to keep on meeting.

*Actor:* I will get this part and stay in town. We can meet over breakfast each week, and help each other know.

*Director:* Then it's settled. We'll keep on getting together as long as we can.

*Actor:* And when we can't?

*Director:* We'll go our separate ways.

## 93

*Actor:* That sounds so final and sad.

*Director:* Should we make promises we don't know if we can keep?

*Actor:* No, that's worse.

*Professor:* But is it really so sad? The love for friends is never final. It travels with us wherever we go.

*Actor:* I wish that were true.

*Professor:* Why wouldn't it be?

*Actor:* We might forget.

*Professor:* Each other? No, I know you don't think that.

*Director:* I agree. But I do have a fear.

*Actor:* What fear?

*Director:* That fame and longing for success will take you away from us, in the end.

*Actor:* But what about you?

*Director:* What about me?

*Actor:* Won't philosophy take you away?

*Director:* It very well may. But I'd try to come back.

*Professor:* That never works.

*Actor:* Why not?

*Professor:* Because philosophy is a deep and fast running river. You can only swim against the flow for so long.

*Actor:* But you can get out of the river and walk or wait on the bank.

*Professor:* The only time a philosopher gets out of the river is right before reaching the sea.

*Actor:* What's the sea supposed to be?

*Professor:* Death.

*Actor:* You mean philosophers aren't ready to die? They have to wait and steady themselves?

*Professor:* No, they're ready. But they want to help prepare others who come down stream.

*Actor:* Is that the idea of philosophy, Director? Standing beside death and helping others prepare?

*Director:* It's one idea, Actor. But not my favorite.

*Actor:* What is your favorite?

*Director:* Helping the wet ones dry off.

*Actor:* So you stay out of the river?

*Director:* No, I swim. But only on hot summer days. And I teach others how to get in, cool down, and get back on their way.

*Actor:* Tell us, Director. Are you ever afraid you'll drown?

*Director:* In ideas? Certainly. It's one of my greatest fears.

*Actor:* I'm afraid of that, too. And you, Professor?

*Professor:* Of course I am. But my students are there to pull me up if I ever start to go down.

*Actor:* My fans do this for me. They often pull me up. What about you, Director?

*Director:* I tend to swim alone.

*Actor:* What if you get tired, or get a cramp?

*Director:* That's the chance I take. I like to go all in.

*Professor:* You're playing for everything you've got.

*Director:* That's how I like to play. And, really, in a way—don't we all?

*Actor:* Hardly. But I go all in. And I know Professor does, too.

*Director:* But Professor has tenure.

*Professor:* What's that supposed to mean? That I don't have the same risk? Even with tenure there are limits to what you can do or say. Director has more freedom of speech than I.

*Actor:* What about me?

*Professor:* You're limited by your fans.

*Actor:* So why does Director have free speech?

*Professor:* Because all they care about is how he does, how business goes with him.

*Actor:* And Director is very good at business.

*Director:* I'd say I'm pretty good.

*Actor:* So you can pretty much say whatever you like?

*Director:* Not quite. There are limits. But fewer than in many other places.

*Actor:* Is that why you're there?

*Director:* That and the money. Don't tell me you two aren't in it at least partially for the money.

*Professor:* The need for money is a limit on our speech.

*Actor:* But I don't really need the money. I have enough.

*Professor:* Then why not make art films instead?

*Actor:* Because I love my fans.

*Director:* You could learn to love the fans of 'art'.

*Actor:* And they could learn to love the 'art' I already make.

*Professor:* While I'd love to talk about this, we really need to get going if we're not to be late.

*Director:* Yes, and I need to find my book then head downtown. Good luck, Artist.

*Actor:* Good luck to you.

*Director:* And good luck to you, Professor.

*Professor:* Thanks. But why do I need luck?

*Director:* Because you have to get your students to focus with Actor in class.

*Professor:* The best of them will treat him like anyone else.

*Actor:* That's all I ask.

*Director:* No, Actor, I think you ask something more. But maybe today will be different.

*Actor:* How so?

*Director:* Instead of seeking approval from them, see if you can't get them to seek it from you.

*Actor:* But it goes both ways.

*Director:* Is that how it goes with you, Professor?

*Professor:* With me it goes neither way. I don't seek approval from them, and I teach them not to seek approval from me.

*Director:* I think that's the better idea.

*Actor:* What do we call this idea?

*Director:* Neither together as one. How's that?

*Actor:* Poetic. And meaningless. But what comes of this idea?

*Director:* Professor?

*Professor:* This really has to be the last word.

*Director:* It's yours.

*Professor:* Freedom.

*Actor:* No! You can't end it on that.

*Professor:* Oh, but I can.

*Actor:* But you have to explain!

*Professor:* Then let's take it up in class.

*Director:* What? What will I be missing?

*Actor:* Too bad business calls you away.

*Director:* Hold on. I'll cancel my meetings and join you—if that's alright with you, Professor.

*Professor:* It's more than alright, Director.

*Actor:* I want the topic of the day to be 'Both Together as One; Neither Together as One—Which is the Better Idea?'

*Director:* What about freedom?

*Actor:* My topic embraces freedom and many other ideas.

*Professor:* We won't have time to cover them all.

*Actor:* Oh, I think we can cover a good amount of ground. All we have to do is do what we did today.

*Director:* What did we do today?

*Actor:* In a word? We played jazz.

*Professor:* Jazz? What, we improvised on a theme?

*Actor:* Exactly!

*Director:* Have you heard the saying 'good enough for jazz'?

*Actor:* I have.

*Director:* What do you think it means?

*Actor:* That jazz isn't too exacting.

*Director:* Why not?

*Actor:* Because the players are laid back and relaxed. But I don't like that saying. Jazz can be the most exacting music of all.

*Director:* How do you like it when you play?

*Actor:* Relaxed and exacting at once.

*Professor:* I didn't know you play jazz.

*Actor:* I don't. I don't like jazz.

*Director:* So you like the idea but not the thing?

*Actor:* Right. I like the idea of jazz but not jazz music itself.

*Professor:* We really need to go.

*Director:* Yes. But I think we have our topic for after class.

*Actor:* What topic?

*Director:* What it means to love an idea but not the idea made real.

*Actor:* Didn't we cover this?

*Director:* We talked about having the wrong idea—with rule, for instance. But what if you have the right idea? And what if you succeed in making it real? And it's terrible for you.

*Professor:* What's terrible is that my students will leave if we're not there in a few minutes.

*Actor:* Here, let me pay for us. We don't have time to split up the bill. You can treat me to dinner. I'd like to go someplace where they play quiet jazz. Quiet so we can talk.

*Director:* Trying to acquire a taste?

*Actor:* I'm trying to set an appropriate scene.

*Professor:* And if you do acquire a taste while setting the scene?

*Actor:* Then that's good.

*Director:* Why?

*Actor:* Because then there's harmony—for us, and me.

Printed in the United States
By Bookmasters